| Vegetarianism

Other Books in the Current Controversies Series

Vegetarianism

Amy Francis, Book Editor

GREENHAVEN PRESS

A part of Gale, Cengage Learning

GALE
CENGAGE Learning·

Farmington Hills, Mich • San Francisco • New York • Waterville, Maine
Meriden, Conn • Mason, Ohio • Chicago

Patricia Coryell, *Vice President & Publisher, New Products & GVRL*
Douglas Dentino, *Manager, New Products*
Judy Galens, *Acquisitions Editor*

For more information, contact:
Greenhaven Press
27500 Drake Rd.
Farmington Hills, MI 48331-3535
Or you can visit our Internet site at gale.cengage.com

Cover image © David Grossman/Alamy.

LIBRARY OF CONGRESS CATALOGING-IN-PUBLICATION DATA

Vegetarianism (Francis) / Vegetarianism / Amy Francis, book editor.
    pages cm. -- (Current controversies)
    Includes bibliographical references and index.
    ISBN 978-0-7377-7227-2 (hardcover) -- ISBN 978-0-7377-7228-9 (pbk.)
    1. Vegetarianism--Juvenile literature. 2. Diet--Moral and ethical aspects--Juvenile literature. 3. Meat industry and trade--Moral and ethical aspects--Juvenile literature. 4. Food preferences--Juvenile literature. I. Francis, Amy. II. Title.
    TX392.V4428 2014
    613.2'6--dc23
                                                                2014026078

Contents

Chapter 1: Are Meat-Based Diets Bad for the Planet?

Yes: Meat-Based Diets Are Bad for the Planet

Although critics argue that demand by vegetarians for high-protein specialty grains, such as quinoa, has lead to human rights abuses, the negative impact of grain production pales in comparison to meat production. The world's farms produce enough grain, legumes, and vegetables to feed the world many times over, but most crops are used for farmed-animal feed. As a result, the continued demand for meat by the wealthy creates a shortage of food for the world's poor.

No: Meat-Based Diets Are Not Bad for the Planet

Chapter 2: What Are the Moral and Spiritual Implications of Vegetarianism?

Chapter 3: Are Vegetarian Diets More Humane than Diets That Include Meat?

Historically many vegetarians cited a belief in nonviolence and spirituality as their motivation for adhering to a vegetarian diet. While more modern vegetarians attribute their choice to health and ecology, there is a resurgence in people devoting themselves to a cruelty-free diet—either one that supports animals being raised in humane conditions or one that avoids animal products all together.

Yes: Vegetarian Diets Are More Humane than Diets That Include Meat

Ethical vegetarians and people who identify as pro-life have much in common. Most vegetarians adopt a meat-free lifestyle out of concern for the welfare animals. It seems then a likely conclusion that these same people would support the pro-life cause, yet neither side seems to see the connection between compassion for animals and for the human unborn.

Gardeners may not be aware that the fertilizers they use come from the same animal factory farms they abhor. There are, however, more ethical alternatives to using animal products when growing produce, such as using plant matter instead of animal by-products for fertilizer.

After MowMar Farms was penalized when workers were seen on video engaging in animal cruelty, the farm industry fought back. It is now illegal to take unauthorized video in these facilities or to document animal cruelty over time to build a case in many meat-industry states. Policing animal farms is now primarily left to the industry to self regulate.

Although many athletes rely on consuming animal products to get the high intake of protein they believe they need for physical fitness, a vegan diet can have a beneficial effect on sports training. Other benefits of veganism include lowered blood pressure, reduced LDL cholesterol and triglycerides, and faster recovery from injury.

The majority of all cases of food poisoning in the United States are attributable, not to meat, but to fruit and vegetables—usually from a virus transmitted on improperly cared-for produce. Of biggest concern is that anyone who comes into contact with food during transport or preparation needs to be alert to and follow proper hygiene.

Foreword

By definition, controversies are "discussions of questions in which opposing opinions clash" (*Webster's Twentieth Century Dictionary Unabridged*). Few would deny that controversies are a pervasive part of the human condition and exist on virtually every level of human enterprise. Controversies transpire between individuals and among groups, within nations and between nations. Controversies supply the grist necessary for progress by providing challenges and challengers to the status quo. They also create atmospheres where strife and warfare can flourish. A world without controversies would be a peaceful world; but it also would be, by and large, static and prosaic.

The Series' Purpose

The purpose of the Current Controversies series is to explore many of the social, political, and economic controversies dominating the national and international scenes today. Titles selected for inclusion in the series are highly focused and specific. For example, from the larger category of criminal justice, Current Controversies deals with specific topics such as police brutality, gun control, white collar crime, and others. The debates in Current Controversies also are presented in a useful, timeless fashion. Articles and book excerpts included in each title are selected if they contribute valuable, long-range ideas to the overall debate. And wherever possible, current information is enhanced with historical documents and other relevant materials. Thus, while individual titles are current in focus, every effort is made to ensure that they will not become quickly outdated. Books in the Current Controversies series will remain important resources for librarians, teachers, and students for many years.

In addition to keeping the titles focused and specific, great care is taken in the editorial format of each book in the series. Book introductions and chapter prefaces are offered to provide background material for readers. Chapters are organized around several key questions that are answered with diverse opinions representing all points on the political spectrum. Materials in each chapter include opinions in which authors clearly disagree as well as alternative opinions in which authors may agree on a broader issue but disagree on the possible solutions. In this way, the content of each volume in Current Controversies mirrors the mosaic of opinions encountered in society. Readers will quickly realize that there are many viable answers to these complex issues. By questioning each author's conclusions, students and casual readers can begin to develop the critical thinking skills so important to evaluating opinionated material.

Current Controversies is also ideal for controlled research. Each anthology in the series is composed of primary sources taken from a wide gamut of informational categories including periodicals, newspapers, books, US and foreign government documents, and the publications of private and public organizations. Readers will find factual support for reports, debates, and research papers covering all areas of important issues. In addition, an annotated table of contents, an index, a book and periodical bibliography, and a list of organizations to contact are included in each book to expedite further research.

Perhaps more than ever before in history, people are confronted with diverse and contradictory information. During the Persian Gulf War, for example, the public was not only treated to minute-to-minute coverage of the war, it was also inundated with critiques of the coverage and countless analyses of the factors motivating US involvement. Being able to sort through the plethora of opinions accompanying today's major issues, and to draw one's own conclusions, can be a complicated and frustrating struggle. It is the editors' hope that Current Controversies will help readers with this struggle.

Introduction

> *"As vegetarian diets and the vegan life-style continue to experience growth, one might expect that [the] social difficulties would improve, but some fear the up-swing of popularity vegetarians and vegans experienced over the last decade might not continue."*

There is no doubt vegetarian diets have enjoyed an increase in popularity over the last decade, but only some vegetarians experience increased social acceptance as a result. Many still have difficulty explaining their choice to family and friends, eating at social functions, and finding things to fulfill their diet—not to mention their hunger—while surveying restaurant menus.

Though the figures vary, the Vegetarian Resource Group puts the number of vegetarians in the United States at a conservative 4 percent of the total population in 2012, up from 2.3 percent in 2006. The food industry has taken notice. From meat and dairy substitutes to prepared frozen vegetarian entrees, evidence of the rise of vegetarianism fills our supermarket shelves. Even vegetarianism's more stringent cousin, veganism, is on the upswing.

According to Angela Haupt, writing for *U.S. News & World Report*, "Vegan diets have lately been surging in popularity, thanks in part to the example of celebrities who are publicly forswearing all animal products."[1] Haupt lists, among others, former president Bill Clinton, actress Michelle Pfeiffer, and

---

1. Angela Haupt, "Me, Give Up Meat? Vegan Diets Surging in Popularity," *U.S. News & World Report*, July 24, 2012. http://health.usnews.com/health-news/articles/2012/07/24/me-give-up-meat-vegan-diets-surging-in-popularity.

singer/songwriter Carrie Underwood as some of the celebrities embracing a vegetarian lifestyle.

Juliet Gellately, director of the vegan and vegetarian group Viva, says there's even been a shift in attitude when it comes to men—traditionally the most resistant group—going vegan. "Before many would say there's no way they'd give up meat. They were traditionalist, loved their steaks and roasts, (and were) macho about it. But now more moneyed, powerful men are coming out and saying vegan is the healthier way."[2]

Add to that initiatives such as Veganuary (Vegan for January) and books like *VB6* (Vegan before 6 o'clock) proclaiming the merits of even part-time veganism for improving everything from health to spiritual growth to Earth's ecology, and it may be hard to imagine anyone experiencing stigma as a result of their food choices. But some still do.

Karen and Michael Iocabbo attribute this disconnect between the popularity of animal-free diets and lack of social acceptance to regional attitudes. They write, "Today vegetarians, depending on which area of the nation they inhabit, feel confident that vegetarianism and even veganism are acceptable. . . . Other vegetarians, those who feel they are the only ones on their blocks or in their small towns, are not as optimistic."[3]

A.G. Sulzberger illustrates this point. He writes in *The New York Times* of his frustration trying to find vegetarian options in restaurants after moving from New York City to the midwest. "In Nebraska . . . vegetarians are sometimes accused of undermining the state economy. The owner of what was billed as the lone vegetarian restaurant in Omaha said it had

---

2. Quoted in Vanessa Barford, "The Rise of the Part-Time Vegans," *BBC News Magazine*, February 17, 2014. http://www.bbc.com/news/magazine-25644903.

3. Karen and Michael Iocabbo, "Vegetarianism in the USA: A Rocky Road," EarthSave, accessed April 14, 2014. http://www.earthsave.org/news/03summer/vegetarianism _usa.htm.

several pounds of ground beef thrown at its doors shortly after opening. After a short run, it closed."[4]

Everything can't be chalked up to regional differences. Nationwide, restaurants seem to be particularly slow to accommodate those wishing to eat animal-free. The animal rights group PETA (People for the Ethical Treatment of Animals) maintains a list of vegan options at fast-food chain restaurants, but most only offer one option and often that is woefully inadequate. For example, PETA's tip for ordering the Veggie Delite at Subway? "Visit the nearest grocery store, purchase some fake lunch meats, and load up your sub!"

According to some reports, more upscale restaurants aren't getting the message either. Jane Fynes-Clinton, writing in *The Courier-Mail*, states, "I may as well have said I carried an infectious disease, so askance were the looks I got from wait staff when I announced myself as the vegetarian mentioned in our New Year's Eve dinner booking. . . . Even today, we vegetarians are too often the pariahs of eating houses and curiosities at social gatherings."[5]

Fynes-Clinton isn't the only one to note challenges in social situations. Laura Frisk, writing for PETA, recounts the difficulties she had with family, friends, and coworkers when she switched to a vegan diet. "They might make fun of you for your food choices, get perturbed when you don't eat the animal-derived products that they prepared for you, or shun you because your vegan lifestyle makes them uncomfortable. . . . I really don't know which was the hardest

---

4. A.G. Sulzberger, "Meatless in the Midwest: A Tale of Survival," *New York Times*, January 10, 2012. http://www.nytimes.com.

5. Jane Fynes-Clinton, "Vegetarianism Debate Should Give Us All Food for Thought," *The Courier-Mail*, January 9, 2014. http://www.couriermail.com.au/news/opinion/opinion-vegetarianism-debate-should-give-us-all-food-for-thought/story-fnihsr9v-1226797636355.

for me: giving up eating animal-derived products or having to explain why I was doing so to all my nonvegan friends and relatives!"[6]

As vegetarian diets and the vegan lifestyle continue to experience growth, one might expect that these social difficulties would improve, but some fear the upswing of popularity vegetarians and vegans experienced over the last decade might not continue. Karen and Michael Iocabbo argue that if history repeats itself, the trend might be just a fad. In the late twentieth century, they explain, "vegetarianism took a dive." It wasn't the science that caused the decline, they say, but the rise in advertising by the meat and dairy industries. They write, "Slowly, ads for meat and milk became ubiquitous. Vegetarians had no advertising budget."[7] In fact, the Worldwatch Institute reported in 2012 that meat production tripled over the previous forty years and increased 20 percent in just the last decade.

Of course, no one knows for certain what the future holds for vegetarianism and veganism and the people who follow their tenets. The authors of the viewpoints in the following pages of *Current Controversies: Vegetarianism* seek to understand what it means today as they explore the following questions: Are meat-based diets bad for the planet? What are the moral and spiritual implications of vegetarianism? Are vegetarian diets more humane than diets that include meat? And is a vegetarian diet beneficial for health?

6. Laura Frisk, "Conquering Difficulties When Going Vegan," PETA Prime, accessed April 14, 2014. http://prime.peta.org/2012/09/difficult.

7. Op. cit.

Are Meat-Based Diets Bad for the Planet?

Overview: People Choose Their Diets Based on Personal Reasons

Stephanie Kraftson, Jana Pohorelsky, and Alex Myong

At the time of this writing, Stephanie Kraftson, Jana Pohorelsky, and Alex Myong were all students at the University of Michigan.

Along with the current trend of eating "organic" and "local" foods, one of the hot topics that has sparked debate among scholars and bloggers alike is the question of whether or not being a vegetarian affects the environment. Those who believe that vegetarianism has a positive effect on the environment argue that the massive production of animal products for human consumption can lead to land degradation, water and air pollution, and even a change in climate. Academic research indicates that these detrimental effects accrue as we continue producing meat products. However, a review of comments from both vegetarian and meat-eating Internet bloggers shows that the human desire for choice—especially choices about the vital need for food—is the most important figure in this debate. To account for those who choose to eat meat despite the benefits of vegetarianism for the environment, the question then remains: how can we make meat-eating more sustainable?

Vegetarianism and the Environment: A Scholarly Look

In 2000, the World Health Organization reported that one in every three people suffered from malnutrition as a result of rapid population growth and diminished land, water, and energy resources. Therefore, in response to the public's increasing concerns about our impact upon the earth's welfare, scientists have begun to research ways in which we can positively influence our environment. Though we often think of vegetarianism as a lifestyle chosen as a result of dietary limitations or desires to protect the health and improve treatment of animals, many people are beginning to ask, "Does vegetarianism actually benefit the environment as well?"

Let's look at the scientific literature: In a 2009 Californian study comparing the environmental effects of vegetarian versus non-vegetarian diets, the researchers sought to answer this question and elaborate upon it by asking, "Does animal consumption create a heavier footprint than a vegetarian diet?" and "If so, what are some of the major environmental effects of an animal-based diet, and how might these be measured?" They found that a non-vegetarian diet consumed 2.9 times more water, 2.5 times more primary energy, 13 times more fertilizer, and 1.4 times more pesticide than a vegetarian diet. These statistics suggest that vegetarian diets are, in fact, less taxing on the environment. These researchers support the notion that increased environmental degradation is a byproduct of increased agricultural output. Modern agriculture has prioritized optimum crop yields and animal farming to the detriment of the environment via increased energy output, use of natural resources, and generation of waste. An Italian study presented in the *European Journal of Clinical Nutrition* that specifically evaluated the environmental impact of omnivorous and vegetarian/vegan diets based on both non-organic and organic products as six separate dietary patterns in addition to a "normal" or average Italian diet produced similar results. Again, the researchers concluded that meat-based diets strain the environment the most and found that water consumption, in particular, plays the most significant role by accounting for 41–46% of the overall impact.

This data raises another question, however: whether vegetarian diets are sufficiently sustainable or are simply more sustainable than animal-based diets—that is, are current vegetarian diets "enough"? The majority of recent studies have focused on the comparison of non-vegetarian and vegetarian diets, but have yet to offer concrete conclusions on the practicality of mass implementation [of] environmentally friendly diets. The *European Journal of Clinical Nutrition* study points to the importance of considering two factors, however: "(1) people generally and openly display extreme reluctance to change their eating habits; (2) a change in the eating habits and in the dietary trends of developing countries may play an important role in the arrest and reversal of some major current environmental trends." If future studies can integrate these suggestions, then perhaps we will come closer to an effective solution to our increasing environmental concerns.

It appears that the voice of opposition is not against vegetarianism, but rather the challenge to the personal choice of eating meat.

What the Bloggers Are Saying

Whether you do a Google search for "vegetarian and environment debate" or "anti-vegetarianism," the popular consensus among bloggers on the Internet seems to be that being a vegetarian does have positive effects on the environment. The question for many, it appears, is not "does being a vegetarian help the environment?" but "how realistic is it to be vegetarian?" and "what is my personal choice to become a vegetarian?" These queries produce more nuanced responses.

If you Google.com "how does being vegetarian help the environment?" the answer from multiple websites resound with some of the following explanations: meat-eating destroys natural habitats, the meat-industry produces greenhouse gases, and raising animals for slaughter leads to an inefficient use of agricultural land. One website, called "chooseveg.com," cites a Dr. David Brubaker of Johns Hopkins University to sum up these consequences of meat consumption: "It pollutes our environment while consuming huge amounts of water, grain, petroleum, pesticides and drugs. The results are disastrous." Even websites that are yielded from a search into "anti-vegetarianism" confirm that maintaining a vegetarian diet is healthy for both the individual and the environment. Anti-vegetarians, such as those who post on the website for the "Anti-Vegetarian Society of Meat-Eaters," don't implicate the environment in their arguments that endorse meat eating. Instead, they focus on the issue of personal liberty to choose to eat meat: "We continue to see activist and political efforts aimed at being the 'Kitchen Police,' telling people what they can and cannot eat." It appears that the voice of opposition is not against vegetarianism, but rather the challenge to the personal choice of eating meat.

Scholars and bloggers appear to agree: human vegetarianism is a healthy option for the environment.

But anti-vegetarianists aren't the only people who call upon the rhetoric of "choice" with regards to eating or not eating meat: many vegetarians weigh in on the debate by addressing environmental concerns while specifying that these were not their primary reason for "going vegetarian." One vegetarian blogger reflecting on his/her own reasons for becoming a vegetarian writes, "I'm a vegetarian for various reasons: the environmental reason would probably be enough for me . . . the most important reason . . . is totally different however. Basically I'm a vegetarian for spiritual reasons." Another vegetarian blogger explains that his/her choice to eat a vegetarian diet is due to the animal cruelty performed by the commercial meat industry so that cheap meat can be produced and consumed. This vegetarian claims, "There are not too many people that are veggie for environmental reasons alone. . . . If that means I contribute less to environmental damage by that choice, so be it." So while environmental issues may be considered important, the emphasis remains on the fact that a variety of personal reasons result in one's choice to become a vegetarian.

Finally, both vegetarians and non-vegetarians on the Internet comment on the reality of choosing not to [eat] meat. Concerns about the relative healthiness of being a vegetarian to that of eating meat are prominent threads on the Internet. Many bloggers comment on whether or not vegetarians receive enough nutrients from their diet (the answer seems to be "yes", as long as they make sure to incorporate foods that are sources of particular nutrients that meat-eaters generally access through meat). As one Internet writer notes, however, "the reality is we have to make [the planet] more sustainable for people who don't want to be vegetarians." He admits that while avoiding meat is highly beneficial to the environment, it is important to recognize that many people will refuse to become vegetarians and that there are ways to make meat eating more sustainable, such as eating less meat and discriminating against certain types of meat—beef in particular. This nuanced argument, which was also offered by academic researchers, offers a practical response to the vegetarian debate.

Thus, scholars and bloggers appear to agree: human vegetarianism is a healthy option for the environment. "Choice" and "reality" seem to be fundamental figures in the debate about vegetarianism and its impact on the environment. According to both the academic and the Internet communities, being a vegetarian does help the environment. But the question remains: how can the choice of human diets—both vegetarian and meat-based—be made more sustainable?

Vegetarians Contribute to Global Food Security

Live58

Live58 is a nonprofit organization whose mission is to end extreme poverty worldwide by 2035.

I don't consider myself a very health-conscious person.

I adore my daily overdose of sugar-infested drinks, and I love eating the occasional high-calorie value meal from McDonald's. Oh, and if there are barbeque chips in your pantry, well, let's just say don't invite me over anytime soon. And, like most Americans, I also enjoy meat. Bacon, hamburger, pork, chicken . . . you name it!

When my older sister became a registered dietician over a year ago, she started to inform my family about our unhealthy eating habits. Her comments weren't annoying or judgmental in any way, yet I still became defensive of my food choices. What's so wrong with the stuff I eat? After all, my weight is still technically considered "normal," and I enjoy consuming food that tastes good.

Then my sister started cooking us meals without meat in them, claiming that being a vegetarian is a healthier way to live.

I was so used to seeing chicken, pork or some kind of beef at every meal that her cooking left me asking, "What is this stuff?"

Even after my sister somewhat succeeded in convincing me that going without animal products is a healthy-lifestyle choice, I still refused to change. No way was I going to be one of those weird plant-loving people who doesn't appreciate a good, juicy steak.

It wasn't until I came to work for Live58 that I finally understood all that being a vegan or vegetarian can mean personally and globally. One of the other interns I work with is a vegetarian and was very open to answering prying questions about her reasons for abandoning the meat-loving world. She is good at spouting off shocking statistics on how becoming a vegetarian can save the environment.

Vegetarianism and Food Security

This got me thinking. If becoming a vegetarian helps save the environment, can it also help eradicate food insecurity?

I did a little research, and I found that the massive amounts of land it takes to grow grain to feed livestock could instead be used to grow food to feed humans. Here are some of the statistics I found:

- The amount of grain produced today is enough to feed the world twice over, but 70 percent of the grain is fed to livestock.

- Meat-manufacturers must feed the animals continuously. Compare that to the amount of food that comes from a dead pig.

- By cycling our grain through livestock, we waste 90 percent of its protein and 96 percent of its calories.

- The feed cost of an 8-ounce steak will fill 45 to 50 bowls with cooked cereal grains.

- The same amount of grain it takes to feed 100 cows could feed 1,000 people.

These facts are shocking. Yet I know that the cause of world hunger is not just about the amount of food being produced. In fact the world already grows enough food to feed every person, so hunger is often caused by other matters such as corrupt governments and inefficient food distribution.

However, I would argue that Westerners are just as guilty as the governments who control their land's resources.

After all, there would not be enough resources for everyone in the world to eat a Western meat-rich diet, so aren't we taking a lot more than our fair share of the earth?

It has been said that it takes about 10 times more land to feed a meat-eater than a vegetarian. If everyone ate less meat, we would be able to use those resources to end extreme poverty.

For now, I am still not a vegetarian, but recently I heard about a movement of becoming what's called a "nearly vegetarian," or "flexitarian." Flexitarians are those who cut meat out of their daily diet, but do not refuse it when it is served to them or when it is the only option. This sounds like the best of both worlds to me.

Part 2: Flexitarians

For the past two weeks, I have embraced the "flexitarian" lifestyle where I don't eat meat during my daily life—other than when it is served to me or is locally raised.

By drastically reducing the amount of meat from my normal diet, I have noticed a tremendous change in how I feel. I have more energy (I have actually started jogging), my digestive system is more regulated and I have even lost a couple of pounds. In no way do I regret my decision to eat less meat.

Can Becoming a Vegetarian End World Hunger?

No. Of course not. I hope my previous [comments] did not lead you to this conclusion. Extreme poverty and world hunger are multi-faceted global problems that are caused by government corruption, a lack of proper food distribution, and other reasons that don't include eating a meaty diet.

But I do believe that it *is* important for consumers to understand what they are purchasing, whether it's meat or other items purchased from the grocery store. Westerners should be mindful of what they are eating and how it gets to their mouths. How do unsustainable animal products affect you and the world as a whole? God has entrusted us to be responsible stewards over His creation, and our bodies are meant to be temples of the Holy Spirit. We should be fulfilling God's purpose in our daily lives, whether that includes Bible reading, prayer, or being conscious consumers.

One way we can be good stewards over creation is through altering our meat eating lifestyle.

By 2050, it is estimated that the earth's population will reach 9 billion. Because 18 percent of all man-made greenhouse gas emissions comes from meat production, we will need to cut our meat consumption by 50 percent in order to feed everyone and to prevent a climate change disaster.

Fertilizers used for grain to feed cattle contain high amounts of nitrous oxide. In fact, growing crops for feeding animals produce more emissions than crop that goes directly into the human food chain.

Giving up meat just even once a week can have a huge effect on the world and on your health.

Becoming a vegetarian can't end world hunger, but altering your meat-eating lifestyle can help future food security.

This does not mean I am pressuring you to go vegan, vegetarian or even flexitarian. According to an article from *The Gaurdian UK*:

The international development select committee said that the increase in meat eating was only one of many factors underlying the global food crises that have afflicted the developing world twice in the last five years, in 2008 and 2011, but going vegetarian even for just a few meals a week is something that most people could manage easily, and with positive health impacts.

I understand that it can be really hard to go without meat, especially because meat is such an inherent part of our Western culture.

However, giving up meat just even once a week can have a huge effect on the world and on your health. A global campaign called Meatless Mondays encourages consumers to give up meat every Monday. The campaign claims that cutting back on meat reduces your risk for cancer, heart disease, diabetes and obesity. It reduces your carbon footprint, water dependence and fossil fuel dependence.

You'll also save money. Consider giving the money you've saved by not purchasing meat to a cause that works to end hunger, like our alliance partner Food for the Hungry.

If you simply can't bear to part with meat at all, I recommend becoming an ethical omnivore. Eat only high-quality meat from non-factory farms. If you only buy grass-fed, hormone-free, locally-raised meat options, you will be creating a new demand for a moral and healthy meat market.

Overall, I believe eating less meat is imperative to food security. Just reducing portion sizes can help.

Meat-Based Diets Perpetuate Global Hunger and Climate Change

Mimi Bekhechi

Mimi Bekhechi is the director of the People for the Ethical Treatment of Animals organization, more commonly known as PETA.

It is ironic that in the wake of the Tesco horse burger scandal [January 2013], writer Joanna Blythman would attempt to scare us off healthy crops such as quinoa and portray meat eaters as eco heroes. Our burgers and bangers hold their share of dark secrets—and they don't just lie in the origin of the animals whose flesh is ground up and extruded into patties and links, although those secrets are plenty dark enough. They also lie in the tremendous waste and environmental havoc wreaked by the meat industry.

Bolivian villagers aren't the only ones faced with the prospect of going hungry. It is estimated that more than 850 million people worldwide do not have enough to eat. But the solution to this crisis does not lie in abstaining from quinoa (whose meteoric rise in popularity cannot be attributed solely to vegans, many of whom have never touched the stuff) and other healthy vegan foods. According to Worldwatch, it is animal agriculture that is the real villain because meat consumption is an inefficient use of grain—the grain is used more efficiently when consumed directly by humans. Growth in meat output requires feeding grain to animals, creating competition for grain between affluent meat eaters and the world's poor.

Global Hunger

With hundreds of millions of hungry people worldwide, it is criminally wasteful to feed perfectly edible food to farmed animals in order to produce meat, rather than feeding it directly to people—especially when you consider that it takes 4.5 pounds of grain to make one pound of chicken meat and 7.3 pounds of grain to produce one pound of pork. Even fish on fish farms are fed up to five pounds of wild-caught fish in order to produce one pound of farmed-fish flesh. This is inefficiency at its worst.

Yes, your beef or pork may be locally grown, but what about the animals' feed? Vegans aren't gobbling up all the soybeans—cattle are. A staggering 97% of the world's soya crop is fed to livestock. It would take 40m [million] tonnes of food to eliminate the most extreme cases of world hunger, yet nearly 20 times that amount of grain—a whopping 760m tonnes—is fed to farmed animals every year in order to produce meat. The world's cattle alone consume enough food to sustain nine billion people, which is what the world's human population is projected to be by 2050.

We have the power to end hunger and save lives—both human and animal—every time we sit down to eat.

Because vegans eat plant foods directly, instead of indirectly eating bushels and bushels of grain and soya that have been funnelled through animals first, even vegans who sometimes eat exotic foods grown in other countries still make a fraction of the impact on the environment that meat eaters do (many of whom also eat exotic foods). Enough food for a vegan can be produced on just one-sixth of an acre of land, while it takes 3¼ acres of land to produce sufficient food for a meat eater. Vegfam, which funds sustainable plant food projects, estimates that a 10-acre farm can support 60 people by growing soybeans, 24 people by growing wheat or 10 people by growing maize—but only two by raising cattle.

According to a United Nations [UN] report, the meat industry is "one of the top two or three most significant contributors to the most serious environmental problems, at every scale from local to global", and the UN has concluded that a global shift towards a vegan diet is vital to save the world from hunger, fuel poverty and the worst impacts of climate change. A study published last October [2012] by the European Commission found that switching to a vegetarian diet results in twice the carbon emissions savings of switching to an electric car.

Aside from their environmental impact, the meat, dairy and egg industries cause immense suffering to more than a billion animals every year in the UK [United Kingdom] alone, most of whom spend their entire lives crammed into dark, filthy sheds. They don't get to breathe fresh air until they are on their way to the abattoir, where many have their throats slit while they are still conscious.

We have the power to end hunger and save lives—both human and animal—every time we sit down to eat. We should take that responsibility with more than a grain of, ahem, quinoa.

Livestock Contributes to Global Warming

Robert Goodland and Jeff Anhang

Robert Goodland is retired from his twenty-three-year position as lead environmental adviser at the World Bank Group. Jeff Anhang is a research officer and environmental specialist at the World Bank Group's International Finance Corporation.

Whenever the causes of climate change are discussed, fossil fuels top the list. Oil, natural gas, and especially coal are indeed major sources of human-caused emissions of carbon dioxide (CO_2) and other greenhouse gases (GHGs). But we believe that the life cycle and supply chain of domesticated animals raised for food have been vastly underestimated as a source of GHGs, and in fact account for at least half of all human-caused GHGs. If this argument is right, it implies that replacing livestock products with better alternatives would be the best strategy for reversing climate change. In fact, this approach would have far more rapid effects on GHG emissions and their atmospheric concentrations—and thus on the rate the climate is warming—than actions to replace fossil fuels with renewable energy.

Livestock are already well-known to contribute to GHG emissions. *Livestock's Long Shadow*, the widely-cited 2006 report by the United Nations Food and Agriculture Organization (FAO), estimates that 7,516 million metric tons per year of CO_2 equivalents (CO_2e), or 18 percent of annual worldwide GHG emissions, are attributable to cattle, buffalo, sheep, goats, camels, horses, pigs, and poultry. That amount would easily qualify livestock for a hard look indeed in the search for ways to address climate change. But our analysis shows that livestock and their byproducts actually account for *at least* 32,564 million tons of CO_2e per year, or 51 percent of annual worldwide GHG emissions.

This is a strong claim that requires strong evidence, so we will thoroughly review the direct and indirect sources of GHG emissions from livestock. Some of these are obvious but underestimated, some are simply overlooked, and some are emissions sources that are already counted but have been assigned to the wrong sectors. Data on livestock vary from place to place and are affected by unavoidable imprecision; where it was impossible to avoid imprecision in estimating any sum of GHGs, we strove to minimize the sum so our overall estimate could be understood as conservative.

Livestock (like automobiles) are a human invention and convenience, not part of pre-human times, and a molecule of CO_2 exhaled by livestock is no more natural than one from an auto tailpipe.

The Big Picture

[According to the FAO] 7,516 million tons of CO_2e per year [is] attributable to livestock, an amount established by adding up GHG emissions involved in clearing land to graze livestock and grow feed, keeping livestock alive, and processing and transporting the end products. We show that 25,048 million tons of CO_2e attributable to livestock have been undercounted or overlooked; of that subtotal, 3,000 million tons are misallocated and 22,048 million tons are entirely uncounted. When uncounted tons are added to the global inventory of atmospheric GHGs, that inventory rises from 41,755 million tons to 63,803 million tons. FAO's 7,516 million tons of CO_2e attributable to livestock then decline from 18 percent of worldwide GHGs to 11.8 percent. Let's look at each category of uncounted or misallocated GHGs:

Breathing. The FAO excludes livestock respiration from its estimate, per the following argument:

> Respiration by livestock is not a net source of CO_2. . . . Emissions from livestock respiration are part of a rapidly cycling biological system, where the plant matter consumed was itself created through the conversion of atmospheric CO_2 into organic compounds. Since the emitted and absorbed quantities are considered to be equivalent, livestock respiration is not considered to be a net source under the Kyoto Protocol. Indeed, since part of the carbon consumed is stored in the live tissue of the growing animal, a growing global herd could even be considered a carbon sink. The standing stock livestock biomass increased significantly over the last decades. . . . This continuing growth . . . could be considered as a carbon sequestration process (roughly estimated at 1 or 2 million tons carbon per year).

But this is a flawed way to look at the matter. Examining the sequestration claim first: Sequestration properly refers to extraction of CO_2 from the atmosphere and its burial in a vault or a stable compound from which it cannot escape over a long period of time. Even if one considers the standing mass of livestock as a carbon sink, by the FAO's own estimate the amount of carbon stored in livestock is trivial compared to the amount stored in forest cleared to create space for growing feed and grazing livestock.

More to the point, livestock (like automobiles) are a human invention and convenience, not part of pre-human times, and a molecule of CO_2 exhaled by livestock is no more natural than one from an auto tailpipe. Moreover, while over time an equilibrium of CO_2 may exist between the amount respired by animals and the amount photosynthesized by plants, that equilibrium has never been static. Today, tens of billions more livestock are exhaling CO_2 than in preindustrial days, while Earth's photosynthetic capacity (its capacity to keep carbon out of the atmosphere by absorbing it in plant mass) has declined sharply as forest has been cleared. (Meanwhile, of course, we add more carbon to the air by burning fossil fuels, further overwhelming the carbon-absorption system.)

Carbon dioxide from livestock respiration accounts for 21 percent of anthropogenic GHGs worldwide.

The FAO asserts that livestock respiration is not listed as a recognized source of GHGs under the Kyoto Protocol, although in fact the Protocol does list CO_2 with no exception, and "other" is included as a catchall category. For clarity, it should be listed separately in whatever protocol replaces Kyoto.

It is tempting to exclude one or another anthropogenic [human-made] source of emissions from carbon accounting—according to one's own interests—on the grounds that it is offset by photosynthesis. But if it is legitimate to count as GHG sources fossil-fuel-driven automobiles, which hundreds of millions of people do not drive, then it is equally legitimate to count livestock respiration. Little or no livestock product is consumed by hundreds of millions of humans, and no livestock respiration (unlike human respiration) is needed for human survival. By keeping GHGs attributable to livestock respiration off GHG balance sheets, it is predictable that they will not be managed and their amount will increase—as in fact is happening.

Carbon dioxide from livestock respiration accounts for 21 percent of anthropogenic GHGs worldwide, according to a 2005 estimate by British physicist Alan Calverd. He did not provide the weight of this CO_2, but it works out to about 8,769 million tons. Calverd's estimate is the only original estimate of its type, but because it involves only one variable (the total mass of all livestock, as all but cold-blooded farmed fish exhale roughly the same amount of CO_2 per kilogram), all calculations of CO_2 from the respiration of a given weight of livestock would be about the same.

Calverd's estimate did not account for the fact that CO_2 from livestock respiration is excluded from global GHG inventories. It also did not account for the GHGs newly attributed to livestock in our analysis. After adding all relevant GHGs to global GHG inventories, the percentage of GHGs attributable to livestock respiration drops from 21 percent to 13.7 percent.

Land. As there is now a global shortage of grassland, practically the only way more livestock and feed can be produced is by destroying natural forest. Growth in markets for livestock products is greatest in developing countries, where rainforest normally stores at least 200 tons of carbon per hectare. Where forest is replaced by moderately degraded grassland, the tonnage of carbon stored per hectare is reduced to 8.

On average, each hectare of grazing land supports no more than one head of cattle, whose carbon content is a fraction of a ton. In comparison, over 200 tons of carbon per hectare may be released within a short time after forest and other vegetation are cut, burned, or chewed. From the soil beneath, another 200 tons per hectare may be released, with yet more GHGs from livestock respiration and excretions. Thus, livestock of all types provide minuscule carbon "piggybanks" to replace huge carbon stores in soils and forests. But if the production of livestock or crops is ended, then forest will often regenerate. The main focus in efforts to mitigate GHGs has been on reducing emissions, while—despite its ability to mitigate GHGs quickly and cheaply—vast amounts of potential carbon absorption by trees has been foregone.

The FAO counts emissions attributable to changes in land use due to the introduction of livestock, but only the relatively small amount of GHGs from changes each year. Strangely, it does not count the much larger amount of annual GHG reductions from photosynthesis that are foregone by using 26 percent of land worldwide for grazing livestock and 33 percent of arable land for growing feed, rather than allowing it to regenerate forest. By itself, leaving a significant amount of tropical land used for grazing livestock and growing feed to regenerate as forest could potentially mitigate *as much as half (or even more) of all anthropogenic GHGs*. A key reason why this is not happening is that reclaiming land used for grazing livestock and growing feed is not yet a priority; on the contrary, feed production and grazing have been fast expanding into forest.

A significant reduction in livestock raised worldwide would reduce GHGs relatively quickly compared with measures involving renewable energy and energy efficiency.

Or suppose that land used for grazing livestock and growing feed were used instead for growing crops to be converted more directly to food for humans and to biofuels. Those fuels could replace one-half of the coal used worldwide, which is responsible for about 3,340 million tons of CO_2e emissions every year. That tonnage represents 8 percent of GHGs in worldwide GHG inventories that omit the additional GHGs assessed by this article, or 5.6 percent of GHGs worldwide when the GHGs assessed in this article are included. If biomass feedstocks are chosen and processed carefully, then biofuels can yield 80 percent less GHGs per unit of energy than coal. Therefore, the extra emissions resulting from using land for livestock and feed can be estimated to be 2,672 million tons of CO_2e, or 4.2 percent of annual GHG emissions worldwide.

Considering these two plausible scenarios, at least 4.2 percent of worldwide GHGs should be counted as emissions attributable to GHG reductions foregone by using land to graze livestock and grow feed.

Methane. According to the FAO, 37 percent of human-induced methane comes from livestock. Although methane warms the atmosphere much more strongly than does CO_2, its half-life in the atmosphere is only about 8 years, versus at least 100 years for CO_2. As a result, a significant reduction in livestock raised worldwide would reduce GHGs relatively quickly compared with measures involving renewable energy and energy efficiency.

We calculate that the increase in livestock products worldwide from 2002 to 2009 accounts for about 2,560 million tons of CO_2e, or 4.0 percent of GHG emissions.

The capacity of greenhouse gases to trap heat in the atmosphere is described in terms of their global warming potential (GWP), which compares their warming potency to that of CO_2 (with a GWP set at 1). The new widely accepted figure for the GWP of methane is 25 using a 100-year timeframe—but it is 72 using a 20-year timeframe, which is more appropriate because of both the large effect that methane reductions can have within 20 years and the serious climate disruption expected within 20 years if no significant reduction of GHGs is achieved. The Intergovernmental Panel on Climate Change supports using a 20-year timeframe for methane.

The FAO estimates that livestock accounted for 103 million tons of methane emissions in 2004 through enteric fermentation and manure management, equivalent to 2,369 million tons of CO_2e. This is 3.7 percent of worldwide GHGs using, as FAO does, the outdated GWP of 23. Using a GWP of 72, livestock methane is responsible for 7,416 million tons of CO_2e or 11.6 percent of worldwide GHGs. So using the appropriate timeframe of 20 years instead of 100 years for methane raises the total amount of GHGs attributable to livestock products by 5,047 million tons of CO_2e or 7.9 percentage points. (Further work is needed to recalibrate methane emissions other than those attributable to livestock products using a 20-year timeframe.)

Other sources. Four additional categories of GHGs adding up to at least 5,560 million tons of CO_2e (8.7 percent of GHGs emissions) have been overlooked or undercounted by the FAO and uncounted in the existing inventory of worldwide GHGs:

First, *Livestock's Long Shadow* cites 2002 FAO statistics as the key source for its 18-percent estimate. From 2002 to 2009, the tonnage of livestock products worldwide increased by 12 percent, which must yield a proportional increase in GHG emissions. Through extrapolation from the FAO's estimate as well as our own, we calculate that the increase in livestock products worldwide from 2002 to 2009 accounts for about 2,560 million tons of CO_2e, or 4.0 percent of GHG emissions.

Second, the FAO and others have documented frequent undercounting in official statistics of both pastoral and industrial livestock. *Livestock's Long Shadow* not only uses no correction factor for such undercounting, but in some sections actually uses lower numbers than appear in FAO statistics and elsewhere. For example, *Livestock's Long Shadow* reports that 33.0 million tons of poultry were produced worldwide in 2002, while FAO's *Food Outlook* of April 2003 reports that 72.9 million tons of poultry were produced worldwide in 2002. The report also states that 21.7 billion head of livestock were raised worldwide in 2002, while many nongovernmental organizations report that about 50 billion head of livestock were raised each year in the early 2000s. If the true number is closer to 50 billion than to 21.7 billion, then the percentage of GHGs worldwide attributable to undercounting in official livestock statistics would likely be over 10 percent.

Third, the FAO uses citations for various aspects of GHGs attributable to livestock dating back to such years as 1964, 1982, 1993, 1999, and 2001. Emissions today would be much higher.

Fourth, the FAO cites Minnesota as a rich source of data. But if these data are generalized to the world then they understate true values, as operations in Minnesota are more efficient than operations in most developing countries where the livestock sector is growing fastest.

Finally, we believe that FAO has overlooked some emissions that have been counted under sectors other than livestock. These emissions add up to at least 3,000 million tons of CO_2e, or 4.7 percent of GHG emissions worldwide.

An effective strategy must involve replacing livestock products with better alternatives, rather than substituting one meat product with another that has a somewhat lower carbon footprint.

First, the FAO states that "livestock-related deforestation as reported from, for example, Argentina is excluded" from its GHG accounting. Second, the FAO omits farmed fish from its definition of livestock and so fails to count GHGs from their life cycle and supply chain. It also omits GHG emissions from portions of the construction and operation of marine and land-based industries dedicated to handling marine organisms destined to feed livestock (up to half the annual catch of marine organisms).

Lastly, the FAO leaves uncounted the substantially higher amount of GHGs attributable to each of the following aspects of livestock products versus alternatives to livestock products:

- Fluorocarbons (needed for cooling livestock products much more than alternatives), which have a global warming potential up to several thousand times higher than that of CO_2.

- Cooking, which typically entails higher temperatures and longer periods for meat than alternatives, and in developing countries entails large amounts of charcoal (which reduces carbon absorption by consuming trees) and kerosene, each of which emits high levels of GHGs.

- Disposal of inevitably large amounts of liquid waste from livestock, and waste livestock products in the form of bone, fat, and spoiled products, all of which emit high amounts of GHGs when disposed in landfills, incinerators, and waterways.

- Production, distribution, and disposal of byproducts, such as leather, feathers, skin, and fur, and their packaging.

- Production, distribution, and disposal of packaging used for livestock products, which for sanitary reasons is much more extensive than for alternatives to livestock products.

- Carbon-intensive medical treatment of millions of cases worldwide of zoonotic illnesses (such as swine flu) and chronic degenerative illnesses (such as coronary heart disease, cancers, diabetes, and hypertension leading to strokes) linked to the consumption of livestock products. Full accounting of GHGs attributable to livestock products would cover portions of the construction and operation of pharmaceutical and medical industries used to treat these illnesses.

A key risk factor for climate change is the growth of the human population, projected to be roughly 35 percent between 2006 and 2050. In the same period, the FAO projects that the number of livestock worldwide will double, so livestock-related GHG emissions would also approximately double (or rise slightly less if all the FAO's recommendations were fully implemented), while it is widely expected that GHGs from other industries will drop. This would make the amount of livestock-related emissions even more unacceptable than today's perilous levels. It also means that an effective strategy must involve replacing livestock products with better alternatives, rather than substituting one meat product with another that has a somewhat lower carbon footprint.

A substantial body of theory, beliefs, and even vested interest has been built up around the idea of slowing climate change through renewable energy and energy efficiency. However, after many years of international climate talks and practical efforts, only relatively modest amounts of renewable energy and energy efficiency have been developed (along with more nuclear- and fossil-energy infrastructure). GHG emissions have *increased* since the Kyoto Protocol was signed in 1992 and climate change has accelerated. However desirable, even major progress in displacing nonrenewable energy would not obviate substantial action to reduce the huge amounts of livestock-related GHGs emissions.

> *Because of the urgency of slowing climate change, we believe that recommending change directly to industry will be more effective than recommending policy changes to governments.*

Action to replace livestock products not only can achieve quick reductions in atmospheric GHGs, but can also reverse the ongoing world food and water crises. Were the recommendations described below followed, at least a 25-percent reduction in livestock products worldwide could be achieved between now and 2017, the end of the commitment period to be discussed at the United Nations' climate conference in Copenhagen in December 2009. This would yield at minimum a 12.5-percent reduction in global anthropogenic GHGs emissions, which by itself would be almost as much reduction as is generally expected to be negotiated in Copenhagen.

Because of the urgency of slowing climate change, we believe that recommending change directly to industry will be more effective than recommending policy changes to governments, which may or may not eventually lead to change in industry. This is true even though industry and investors normally thrive when they are responsive to customers and shareholders in the short term, while climate seems to pose longterm risks.

Livestock-related GHGs could be managed by governments through the imposition of carbon taxes (despite opposition from the livestock industry), in which case leaders in the food industry and investors would search for opportunities that such carbon taxes would help create. In fact, they might seek to benefit from such opportunities even in the absence of carbon taxes because livestock-related GHG emissions are a grave risk to the food industry itself. Disruptive climate events are forecast to threaten developed markets increasingly, and to result in even more harm to emerging markets, where the food industry is otherwise forecast to achieve its greatest growth.

Meat Production Can Benefit the Earth

Doug Boucher et al.

Doug Boucher and his coauthors of the following viewpoint—Pipa Elias, Lael Goodman, Calen May-Tobin, Kranti Mulik, and Sarah Roquemore—are members of the Union of Concerned Scientists.

Plant production is the most efficient of all, but some kinds of meat production are much more efficient than others, creating opportunities for continued growth in meat consumption while causing much less deforestation.

There are fundamental biological reasons why meat production requires more land and resources than plant production, related to the fact that meat consumption occurs at a higher level on the food chain than plant consumption. When we eat a certain number of calories' worth of steak, we are consuming not only those calories but also, in effect, all the calories consumed by the cow that produced the steak (i.e., the calories in all the food it processed during its lifetime). Producing all the food the cow ate—pasture grasses, feed grains, soy supplements, and forages like alfalfa—requires a great deal of land. For a given amount of energy, it would take far fewer calories and less total land if you were to eat the grain and soy directly rather than feed it to the cow to make the steak. A diet primarily based on meat consumption requires far more land than a vegetarian diet.

Benefits of Meat Production

Despite the greater land use needed to eat higher on the food chain, there are benefits to meat consumption. First, meat is higher in protein than most plants, so you do not need to eat as much to get the amount of protein necessary for a healthy diet. Second, livestock often eat things that humans cannot (or do not) directly consume: cattle eat grass, poultry eat insects (as well as grains and fruits), and pigs will eat just about anything. This allows us to produce food from land and resources that would otherwise be unusable. Cattle, for instance, are able to gain sustenance from large areas of rangeland in arid regions that are not suitable for crop production. Further, livestock offer a store of wealth and a form of food security in regions where crop production is inconsistent. Meat production uses land both directly and indirectly. The direct use is the land that the animals live and graze on. For cattle, sheep, and goats, this land has traditionally been pastures (human-created grasslands) and rangelands (natural ecosystems used for grazing, such as shrublands and savannas). Pigs and chickens have used the same kind of land, but much less of it, staying closer to the farmhouse and often spending most of their time in the farmyard.

Cattle, pigs, and chickens all produce meat, but in doing so they are very different animals.

In addition, animals use land indirectly—through the land used to produce feed and forage for them. "Feed" means grains such as corn, and protein-rich seeds such as soybeans, that are used in supplements; "forage" is other plant matter, such as alfalfa and hay grasses, that is grown in fields, then cut and brought in to feed the livestock in farmyards and barns. Feed and forage cost time and energy to produce and harvest, but they have two advantages: they are considerably higher in protein and energy than the plants in pastures, and they concentrate the food in one place, making it possible for the livestock to satisfy their needs without a lot of movement to find and consume the most edible plants and plant parts. This means that the land that livestock use indirectly is actually used more efficiently than the land they use directly.

Pastures have higher productivity for meat production than does range. Pastures are found in moister climates, they are planted with high densities of faster-growing and more-edible (for cattle) grasses, and they benefit from added inputs such as fertilizer. Pastureland could also be used for crop production, such as cereal grains for bread or pasta, or for animal feed.

Not All Animals Are the Same

Cattle, pigs, and chickens all produce meat, but in doing so they are very different animals. Cattle, sheep, and goats are ruminants; their digestive system includes a section called the rumen, which is home to a prodigious variety of bacteria and other microbes that can break down cellulose, the molecule that makes up the largest proportion of plant matter. Thus ruminants are able to eat cellulose—something that most other animals can do only poorly or not at all. Because most living plant matter on earth is cellulosic, much more of the biosphere's total productivity is potentially available to ruminants as food than to non-ruminant animals (including humans).

This ability to digest cellulose is the reason why ruminants are able to survive and produce meat, although not very efficiently, when eating rangeland plants. Pigs, chickens, and other non-ruminant livestock cannot do this. However, on better-quality agricultural land, including the areas that could potentially be used either as pasture or as cropland, the advantage shifts to pigs and chickens. There are two main reasons for this.

First, the digestive efficiency of the smaller livestock animals is considerably higher. They convert more of their food into edible meat than ruminants, especially cattle. Non-ruminants' diets need to have foods richer in protein, sugars, starches, and fats, but they convert these foods into meat more quickly, and in considerably higher proportions relative to the amounts that they eat, than ruminants. Chickens need to consume two kilograms of grain to produce one kilogram of meat, and pigs need four kilograms, but for beef cattle the ratio is 10 to 1.

Second, land that is good enough to be used either as pasture for ruminants or as cropland to produce grain for pigs and chickens will yield much more edible feed, and of higher quality, when producing grain.

Ruminants need six hectares of land to produce a kilogram (kilo) of protein, while pork production needs only 3.6 hectares.

Thus ruminants are less-efficient meat producers than non-ruminants. This lower efficiency of ruminants means they produce more waste products, just as lower-mileage cars tend to emit more pollutants. Less of what they eat is turned into meat on their bodies, while more remains undigested and becomes waste. Often those waste products can have very negative effects on the environment. For example, the microbes that digest cellulose in the rumen (particularly the multi-billion-year-old types known as Archaea) also produce methane, a potent heat-trapping gas that exits the cow from both ends and causes about 23 times as much global warming per molecule as carbon dioxide. Moreover, the large amounts of manure produced by cattle are both a leading cause of water pollution and an additional source of methane, causing even more global warming.

Overall, given the differences in productivity among livestock animals and the lands that produce most of their food, pigs and especially chickens are much more efficient meat producers than beef cattle. They use much less land to produce an equal amount of protein. This has been measured in several scientific studies, and the differences, reviewed recently by [M.] deVries and [I.J.M.] deBoer (2010), are consistently large.

Here are just a few examples. [S.] Wirsenius, [F.] Hedenus, and [K.] Mohlin (2010) found that it takes about nine hectares of permanent pasture plus about three hectares of cropland to produce one ton of beef. This compares with less than one hectare, almost all cropland, to produce one ton of poultry or pork. As their study focused on the European Union, where pasture productivity is high, the authors' results were not affected by the use of low-quality rangeland in cattle production; the differences they showed involved lands of comparably high quality.

Similarly, [E.] Stehfest et al. (2009) calculated that ruminants need six hectares of land to produce a kilogram (kilo) of protein, while pork production needs only 3.6 hectares. A totally vegetarian alternative using beans, peas, or other legumes reduces this area to 2.7 hectares; no estimate was given for chicken production.

Looking at feed consumption, [V.] Smil (2002) calculated that beef cattle needed to consume 31.7 kilos of total feed to produce one kilo of edible meat, compared with 13.7 kilos of feed for pork and just 4.2 kilos for chickens. Beef cattle converted only 5 percent of the protein in their diet into edible meat, versus 13 percent for pork, 25 percent for chicken, and 30 percent for egg production.

These are just a few examples of what is a consistent pattern. The 2010 review by deVries and deBoer of 16 different studies shows how researchers have found that beef generally requires several times as much land as the alternatives. These studies were all done in developed (Organisation for Economic Co-operation and Development [OECD]) countries in order to avoid the effects of differences in production techniques or land quality, and the results are expressed in terms of land needed to produce a kilo of protein to avoid the bias that would come from comparing foods with different amounts of water (e.g., milk vs. beef). . . . Beef generally requires several times as much land to produce the same amount of protein as the alternatives.

> [There are] several alternatives that would reduce the pressure for deforestation caused by global meat production. Most of these alternatives would also reduce the impact of meat on the global climate.

Beef makes up about 24 percent of the world's meat consumption; poultry accounts for about 34 percent and pork more than 40 percent, with much smaller amounts coming from other sources such as lamb, goat, and guinea pig, as well as bushmeat. But in terms of protein, less than 5 percent of what humanity consumes comes from beef, and in terms of calories, less than 2 percent. Beef cattle produce this meat using about 30 million square kilometers (km^2) of land—27 million of that for grazing, and the rest for the feed and forage they eat, while pork and poultry take less than 2 million km^2 each.

All in all, then, one way to reduce the global demand for agricultural land, and thus decrease the pressure to expand pasture and croplands for feed at the expense of tropical forests, would be to shift our meat consumption toward the more efficient sources. The best candidates are dairy, pork, or chicken. Global trends are already moving in this direction, but a variety of policies could speed them up.

Alternatives to Current Production and Consumption Patterns

Global meat production is projected to approximately double—to 465 Mmt [million metric tons]—in 2050, with the majority of the increase expected in developing countries. As demand for livestock products grows and the sector expands, land requirements for producing livestock will also grow, competing for land with other kinds of food production and with crops grown for bioenergy. However, based on the information summarized in previous sections, we can describe several alternatives that would reduce the pressure for deforestation caused by global meat production. Most of these alternatives would also reduce the impact of meat on the global climate, and some would also bring important benefits to our health.

Lowering overall meat consumption would have beneficial impacts on health and health care costs.

One way to meet this heightened demand is to increase the productivity of land already being used and thereby reduce the need for expansion into forests. This option is sometimes called intensification, and we use this word here simply to mean increasing yield per hectare, without any implication that it involves increased inputs, genetic modification, or other means. In particular, it does not mean moving to production systems based on confined animal feeding operations (CAFOs), which have considerable disadvantages from an environmental point of view. Higher stocking rates (more cattle per hectare of pasture), more productive pastures, rotational grazing, and the use of breeds suited to tropical conditions are some of the ways to increase land productivity. The Brazilian research and extension service EMBRAPA *(http://www.embrapa.br/english)*, for example, has shown that with improved pasture grass mixtures, rotational grazing, weeding, and improved cattle breeds, average stocking rates in the wet tropics could be increased from 1.1 animals per hectare to two or three. As deforestation in the Brazilian Amazon has declined, there is not as much cheap forestland newly available for cattle pasture, giving these kinds of practices an increasing advantage.

With moderate investments, it is possible to raise cattle on abandoned and inexpensive land where grass is already growing, although necessarily with some sacrifice of yield. Other options include supporting more sustainable grazing systems such as silvo-pastoralism, which can increase livestock production and at the same time protect soil against nutrient depletion, compaction, and erosion. What these kinds of alternatives have in common is that they use previously cleared land for expansion, and they adopt production systems that improve the health of the land rather than degrade it.

Another alternative to help move the meat industry toward zero deforestation is to reduce overall meat consumption. While this objective runs counter to the general trend of increasing meat consumption in recent decades, there have been signs of a reduction in some countries, particularly the wealthier ones. There has been a 15 percent drop in Germany, for example, and a 10 percent drop in France.

The negative effects of high levels of meat consumption on health are well documented. These impacts include higher risks of cardiovascular disease, diabetes, obesity, and certain kinds of cancer, as well as greater numbers of premature deaths. Thus, lowering overall meat consumption would have beneficial impacts on health and health care costs.

How much could the demand for land, and thus the pressure for deforestation and the amount of global warming pollution, be reduced by this alternative? One way to gauge the outcome is to first look at the extreme case: what would be the effects of hypothetical total shifts in consumption—eliminating all beef, all other meat, or even all animal products consumed worldwide? [E.] Stehfest et al. calculated that reducing beef consumption to zero by 2050 would cut the need for pasture by 27 million km^2, an 80 percent reduction, as well as reduce the need for cropland. Eliminating all meat consumption would have the same impact on the need for pasture, and eliminating all animal products (including milk and eggs) would reduce pasture needs by a further 5 million km^2. Eliminating ruminant meat would cut agricultural heat-trapping emissions nearly in half; eliminating all meat would reduce emissions a further 6 percent, and eliminating all animal products would cut emissions another 12 percent beyond that. Stehfest et al. used scenarios in which the meat reductions were compensated for by increased consumption of plant protein, rather than by switching to dairy or other kinds of meat.

[J.A.] Foley et al. and Foley also looked at the possibilities of increasing food supply through diet shifts, and found the gain to be very large. They calculated that the world could increase its supply of food calories by 50 percent—a staggering 3 quadrillion calories per year—by shifting to an all-plant diet. This would be a drastic change, but they also recommended looking at diet changes that retain meat consumption, such as shifting from beef to more chicken and pork.

Shifting Meat Consumption to More Land-Efficient Kinds of Meat

As noted earlier, even in Europe where land productivity is high, it takes nine hectares of pastureland and three hectares of cropland to produce one ton of beef. In contrast, it takes only one hectare of cropland to produce a ton of pork or chicken. In tropical countries, where beef production is mostly pasture-based, the land required to produce a ton of beef is even higher. Thus, shifting consumption from beef toward pork and especially poultry would be a good way to reduce the pressure for more land.

Several aspects of this alternative are worth underscoring. Because chickens turn grain into meat more efficiently than beef cattle, there would not only be a savings of grazing land but also of the cropland needed to produce feed grains. The shift would be of considerable help in terms of global warming, as methane emissions from non-ruminants are much lower than those from ruminants such as cattle.

[A.F.] Bouwman et al., studying human alteration of the nitrogen and phosphorus cycles, modeled the impact of a 10 percent shift of beef consumption to poultry, and found that it would reduce fertilizer use, manure production, and the surplus of nitrogen that is a source of pollution. They also noted that this option would be most appropriate for countries with intensive production of ruminants and intensively managed grasslands (i.e., developed countries).

One strong argument for this kind of diet change relates to feasibility. Such a switch would be consistent with current trends in developed and developing countries alike toward increased per capita chicken and pork consumption relative to beef. In developing countries, this change reflects only a slower rate of growth for beef, but in developed countries per capita beef consumption is already declining in absolute terms.

One of the drivers of this trend is the health advantage of reducing beef consumption. A very large, 20-year-long study has strongly confirmed this advantage recently, and eating less beef is now part of official dietary recommendations in countries such as the United States and the United Kingdom. While a recent review assessed beef consumption as being "possibly" or "probably" associated with increasing coronary heart disease as well as higher rates of breast, colon, and prostate cancer it found that poultry consumption is associated with reduced rates of two of these illnesses and "probably no relation" to the other two. In other words, there could be benefits both from the reduction in beef consumption and also from the increase in poultry consumption.

Cattle Can Be Used to Reverse Global Warming

Adam D. Sacks

Adam D. Sacks is executive director of the Center for Democracy and the Constitution.

> Global climate change and land degradation have to be put on a war footing internationally—meaning that all nations need to pull together and treat this threat as we would a war.... Only through uniting and diverting all the resources required to deal with climate change and land degradation can we avert unimaginable tragedy. We have all the money we need. *All we cannot buy is time.*
>
> *Allan Savory*

I've been a climate activist since the millennium turned, twelve long years ago. It's been an eternity of global-warming days since then. I've rallied, marched, petitioned, organized, lectured, blogged, fumed, despaired, studied, argued and hoped. I've met leading lights—scientists, writers, and activists—and took their inspiration into the world, signing onto the party line and fully committing to our collective, world-saving goal: reducing greenhouse gas emissions. And now I wonder if all of our work has made any difference at all.

A Failure

Despite our passion and desperation, Copenhagens and "Inconvenient Truths," despite circuses ("conferences" or "summits" in more polite circles) in Rio, Bali, Copenhagen and elsewhere, despite the increasingly desperate warnings from thousands of scientists studying climate every which way from

Sunday, we've stood by helplessly as the rate of greenhouse gas emissions has steadily *increased*, as the climate has grown hotter and wilder by the year.

It seems that so far we've been unable to come to terms with a painful reality:

Our fight against global warming has not worked.

What I mean by "work" is quite simple: the atmospheric concentration of greenhouse gases falls steadily and surely towards pre-industrial levels of around 280 parts per million (ppm), and doesn't stop until we get there. If we settle for anything less we are just kidding ourselves straight into a hellfire, chaotic and deadly world.

National governments have clearly failed to do their job in addressing climate, and climate chaos is taking over today, not in some distant future.

And that's exactly where we've been heading ever since leading NASA [National Aeronautics and Space Administration] climate scientist Jim Hansen stood up before Congress in 1988 and announced that we're in deep climate trouble. Since then, in the largest coordinated scientific investigation ever, we've confirmed our worst fears by studying everything from ice cores to sea-surface temperatures to sediment samples and ancient layers of rock, to jet streams, gulf streams, to floral and faunal migrations, to ocean chemistry and a universe of other specialties.

Climate activists and writers have worked 24 x 7 as well, aiming at raising public awareness, applying political thumbscrews, creating movements, locally, nationally, anywhere and everywhere. We've threatened, cajoled, manipulated (a.k.a. "social marketing"), called up all the shows of dogs and ponies, rallied, taught-in, partied, networked, and spelled out "350" in a thousand picturesque ways.

So far, not so good.

Governments and Gas Companies

National governments have clearly failed to do their job in addressing climate, and climate chaos is taking over today, not in some distant future. Can we admit that we've not only lost the battle against the Inconvenient Truth, but that the war itself is hanging in the balance? When do we finally figure out that perhaps we are on the wrong path? Here's the problem:

We're obsessed *with greenhouse gas emissions.*

Yes, those greedy oil, gas and coal companies should be stopped. And let's take the cotton-mouthed corporate media to task while we're at it. . . . Unfortunately, right now we are hooked on hydrocarbons and there is no way we're going to kick the habit *in time* without incalculable suffering for millions if not billions of people: no food, no water, no power, no heat, no transportation.

Human greenhouse gas emissions are much more than the gases from our tailpipes and power plants. They're also the gases from the melting permafrost and seabed floor, from the failing carbon sinks of dying forests, warming oceans and wilderness sacrificed to agriculture. In fact, the soils destroyed worldwide by humans since the advent of agriculture have added more than twice the greenhouse gases to the atmosphere than all emissions from fossil fuels.

And there's more to come, in the form of self-sustaining positive feedback loops that will surge ahead with no further help from us. For example, melting permafrost contains twice as much carbon as the atmosphere, and as it emits carbon over the years it will warm the atmosphere further and continue to accelerate its own melting and emissions.

Here we are: the elephant has arrived in the room, special delivery. The elephant is *bigger* than the room. Of course we should stop the carbon machine, marshal everything in our power to do so, but we'd better recognize that we're not doing it, and we've got to do something else as well. Something very big. Because the fact is that we can't stop, or even reduce, this global civilization's greenhouse gas emissions *in time*.

Grazing animals are the path to restoration of the world's grasslands, which has the potential to pull all of the legacy carbon out of the atmosphere and put it back into the ground where it belongs.

That's not, "*Maybe* we won't stop this global civilization's greenhouse gas emissions *in time*." It's not "We *probably* won't stop this global civilization's greenhouse gas emissions *in time*." It's "We *can't* stop this global civilization's greenhouse gas emissions *in time*." We have proved this to ourselves beyond a shadow of a doubt, even if we refuse to admit it: CANNOT. If we had the luxury of a leisurely pace, sure, we would eventually reduce emissions, but time is precisely what we don't have.

A Fix

Our first priority is to get greenhouse gases out of the atmosphere and into the ground as rapidly as possible.

And now here's the good—and surprising—news: All we need is dirt. And cows.

Grazing animals are the path to restoration of the world's grasslands, which has the potential to pull all of the legacy carbon out of the atmosphere and put it back into the ground where it belongs. And keep it there for thousands of years. It's a most convenient truth.

We have evidence to indicate that, in three decades or less, it is possible to return greenhouse gases to the climate-stable pre-industrial levels of 280 ppm. It requires no unknown or complicated technology—in fact, no technology at all. It is based on nature's brilliant soil-based carbon capture and storage, also called Holistic Management of grasslands. It has so many benefits—including an eventual net cost of zero or less—that even if climate weren't an issue we should be doing it anyway.

In general, to the extent we've already considered carbon capture and storage, the focus has been on expensive high-tech engineering schemes which, like all high-tech schemes are fraught with potentially catastrophic unintended consequences. Global warming itself is an unintended consequence of technology, the Mother of Unintended Consequences, and like all of them was impossible to anticipate.

Thanks to an innovative Zimbabwean biologist and rangeland manager named Allan Savory, for decades we've been learning how to restore desertified grasslands by re-establishing the evolutionary relationship between grazing animals and their habitats. So far this has been accomplished on 40 million acres across Africa, South America, Australia and the U.S.

What we need for returning to pre-industrial atmospheric carbon levels is within ready reach: billions of acres of plains and savannas—mostly damaged by improper human use—and billions of grazing animals, managed the way nature has successfully done it for millions of years. This is the polar opposite of conventional livestock management, where animals are left to overgraze and turn the land to mud and dust. Confusion over the categorical differences between the two approaches has resulted in misleading assessments that lead us in precisely the wrong direction.

There is no climate-saving strategy that has anywhere near the potential of soils.

Unknown to most climate folks, there are mainstream scientific studies that show the enormous carbon storage capacity of soils (where there is currently more than twice the carbon than in the atmosphere). Capturing one ton of carbon per acre per year is a reasonable expectation on conventionally well-cared for grasslands, even without the benefit of animals that break capped soil surfaces with their hooves, fertilize, moisturize and aerate the ground, and make earth hospitable to thousands of vital soil organisms. Add proper management of cattle, goats, sheep and other grazers, the soil-based carbon capture and storage potential increases dramatically (while under conventional rangeland management soils lose carbon every year).

Another confusion for climate activists is that they want CO_2 numbers, whereas rangeland activists are satisfied when they *see* the carbon in the soil: healthy dirt is black (the color of carbon), soft, moist, brimming with microbial, fungal, green plant, insect and animal life, resilient to droughts and floods. But because such evidence, powerful though it is, is unfamiliar to the climate crew, we have trouble grasping how effective soil carbon sequestration can be. As a result, there is untoward resistance to soil-based carbon capture and storage among global warming warriors. It is difficult for us to believe that a traditional climate enemy, cows, are our friends.

Yet there is no climate-saving strategy that has anywhere near the potential of soils. There are roughly 12 billion acres worldwide, mostly ruined by human misuse, which we can restore. At a modest one ton per acre we can pull twelve billion tons of carbon out of the atmosphere every year. That's 6 parts per million (ppm)—and even if we foolishly continue to add 2 ppm annually, it's still less than a 30-year trip back to a stable preindustrial 280 ppm, down from today's perilous 393.

Early on we may have been right to pursue the obvious—reducing emissions—and for a while it even seemed that it might work. But it hasn't, and after all these years of habit we resist aiming our activism elsewhere. Here's an example, starring a climate hero.

During winter 2010, a restoration ecologist, a rangelands activist and I drove from Boston up to Middlebury College in snowy Vermont to visit Bill McKibben, urging him to investi-

gate grassland restoration. He was convinced enough to research and write an article about it—and a good one at that:

> Done right, some studies suggest, this method of raising
> cattle could put much of the atmosphere's oversupply of
> greenhouse gases back in the soil inside half a century. That
> means shifting from feedlot farming to rotational grazing is
> one of the few changes we could make that's on the same
> scale as the problem of global warming ("The Only Way to
> Have a Cow," *Orion* magazine, March/April 2010, http://
> www.orionmagazine.org/index.php/articles/article/5339/).

He even spoke at a conference held by the Quivira Coali-
tion, an organization dedicated to eco-restoration in the
American west. But since then, even though he appears to be
in agreement . . . silence.

Why only one mention of soil-based carbon capture and
storage, a minimal aside, on 350.org? McKibben has been
waging a noble battle against fossil fuels and writing about the
associated politics and economics for decades, yet our pre-
dicament is more dire than ever. At this point perhaps it is
time for him and the rest of us to stop, catch our breaths (and
lick our wounds), regroup and rethink.

---

*What we would need are the already abundant lands
that have been abused unto uselessness, some eager and
dedicated ranchers and herders, and some ruminating
animals.*

On the plus side, in 2010 the Africa Centre for Holistic
Management in Zimbabwe won the $100,000 Buckminster
Fuller Award for its "proposal that has significant potential to
solve humanity's most pressing problems." At the time of this
writing, January 2013, the Savory Institute is one of eleven fi-
nalists out of 2,600 applicants in business magnate Richard
Branson's $25 million Virgin Earth Challenge. The Challenge's

goal is to advance "the successful commercialisation of ways of taking greenhouse gases out of the atmosphere and keeping them out with no countervailing impacts." Branson's concept is flawed: what if saving the climate is *not* commercially viable? Does that mean we *shouldn't* do it? How commercially viable is a dead civilization? But $25 million would help eco-restoration along, and despite a faulty premise it is still possible to do the right thing.

More on the plus side: along with massive carbon sequestration, global-scale restoration of grasslands re-establishes a balanced hydrological cycle, soil integrity and biodiversity; helps stabilize local and, eventually, global weather patterns; provides positive stable work opportunities, particularly in third-world countries; produces high-quality animal protein without synthetic soil supplements and destructive factory farming; and supports local communities worldwide in sustainable living.

The icing on the eco-cake? We would need far less along the lines of slow and barely more than symbolic international agreements, endless contorted and protracted government approvals, complex machinery, dangerous geo-engineering experiments, or prohibitive sums of taxpayer money thrown at desperate and wacky technologies. What we would need are the already abundant lands that have been abused unto uselessness, some eager and dedicated ranchers and herders, and some ruminating animals. These are readily available and, as far as rescuing life on earth for future millennia goes, pretty cheap—far less than the cost of recovering from just one super-hurricane like Sandy.

The New Focus

Put carbon back into the ground. Now.

Suppose that just some of the efforts currently dedicated to emissions reduction were shifted to eco-restoration and biologically-based carbon sequestration in soils. Instead of endlessly pleading with government and industry, suffocating in bureaucracy and political quagmires, arguing about profits and tax breaks, we just hit the ground—grazing. Imagine if 350.org dedicated some of its global efforts to turn communities to carbon farming. Or if officials and commercial operations started setting aside currently useless rangelands for restoration of grasses, water cycles, and soils, and producing jobs and high-quality protein. And while worldwide international agreement would be a wonderful thing, we can proceed without it—even a relatively small group of people could do the job, and it would be hard to mount objections to restoring ruined land that is currently bereft of healthy biodiversity, barely useful for anything else.

There's plenty of money out there to redirect towards saving life on earth.

You don't even have to believe that global warming exists, only that healthy soils are beneficial. Who knows, maybe it's even possible to unite climate skeptics with firebrands, profiteers with non-profiteers, corporations with real, live people. I would venture that not many folks prefer parched, cracked, lifeless earth to fields of waving grasses, full of creatures great and small.

We can get together on this one.

It would make sense for governments to step forward, since public coffers already supply a lion's share of the cash to *undo* what carbon economies have wrought: Hurricane Katrina cost the U.S. taxpayers around $110 billion, Hurricane Sandy likely upwards of $50 billion. And that's just the tip of the iceberg (if we can find one).

There's plenty of money out there to redirect towards saving life on earth. What about the $1 trillion in annual worldwide subsidies to the fossil fuel industries? Or the $396 billion price tag on America's F-35 jet (with a projected long-term cost of $1,100,000,000,000), a single over-budget weapons system, designed to fight threats not a fraction as threatening as our current path to a climate-ravaged planet.

While we should at least make an effort to aim national treasuries at survival strategies, here's another proposal as well: big bucks from the coal, oil and gas industry.

Is it a good idea? Would supporting soil sequestration just wind up as an excuse to keep pumping out carbon, or creating bogus "carbon credits"? Maybe. But, since no excuses have been needed yet, why would fossil mongers need one now? In any case, given the current accelerating climate death spiral, desperate measures are in order. Besides, that obsolete breed of capitalists may have reasons of their own to agree, not the least of which is that there aren't very many customers on a starving planet, burned to a crisp.

Of course we should do everything we can to keep carbonaceous fuels deep in the ground. Given our dismal track record, however, and the pressing state of emergency, let's move ahead on eco-restoration with all due dispatch, and let the corporate purveyors of pollution help pay for it.

Pull out all the stops and put carbon back into the ground—the way nature does it.

Will soil sequestration of carbon do everything to save us? In and of itself, unfortunately not. We need to restore forest and other ecosystems as well, expand our understanding of how nature cycles carbon, and apply it. Furthermore, we're still confronted by a growing and hungry population, depleted resources, species extinctions, inequity and many other afflictions of civilization. But if we don't solve global warming all of our other problems will be moot.

Savory was absolutely correct: the only thing we cannot buy is time. Never was there a more urgent need to prepare for war. Never was there to be a war which would build, not destroy, and which would save so many lives. And to that point restoration of grasslands is so far ahead of anything else on the table, in a wealth of ways, that a failure to embrace it—with all due dispatch, with all necessary resources—would be tragic.

Grazing Animals Improve
Soil Quality

Heather Dugmore

Heather Dugmore is a journalist based in Johannesburg, South Africa. She is also the coauthor of Muthi and Myths from the African Bush.

"A universal fear of running livestock in large numbers is the biggest cause of veld deterioration, soil erosion and desertification in the world. I said so 50 years ago, and I say it again with urgency, that hoof action, with an emphasis on large livestock hooves, is the secret to restoring degraded landscapes. They work the soil better than any machine can possibly do, and healthy soil creates healthy vegetation.

"Outdated notions of endlessly resting the land and decreasing animal numbers will accelerate our downfall." Zimbabwean-born Allan Savory makes an impassioned plea for the world's soils and grasslands. Now in his 70s, Allan is as committed to healing the veld as he was five decades ago. More than 70 farmers from throughout South Africa attended his three-day workshop in Graaff-Reinet in mid-April [2012], and many others had to be turned away for lack of space.

Finally, his message is being heard. From the United Nations to farmers all over the world, Allan's call for a Brown Revolution, which focuses on what we are doing to the soil, is taking hold. "The soil is the greatest storage space for carbon and fresh water; greater than all the dams, lakes and rivers in the world, but we have messed it up," Allan explains.

To restore healthy soil to the seasonally humid and dry grasslands of the world requires substantial numbers of large herbivores on the land, tightly herded together, grazing, trampling, dunging and urinating on a piece of land and then moving on after a brief period, just as the great wildlife herds once did. In most parts of the world those herds are gone, and we now need to use livestock, particularly cattle, to achieve what Allan calls "herd effect, animal impact and hoof action."

"Soils, plants and animals developed together and need to be managed together in a socially, environmentally and economically sound manner. Holistic farming sets out to achieve this," continues Allan. "This is not a modern concept. French biochemist and farmer André Voisin published evidence, 60 years ago, that overgrazing of plants was not related to animal numbers, contrary to what mainstream rangeland scientists believe. He showed that grazing and plant recovery related to time; the number of days the plants are grazed and the number of days before they are grazed again."

It has been an uphill battle for Allan [Savory] to demonstrate the wisdom of what is now known as holistic farming, holistic range management or holistic veld management.

Holistic Farming

Allan explains that a primary principle of holistic farming is to time the grazing and restoration periods to achieve maximum soil and plant biodiversity and vigour. Using holistic planned grazing, farmers are able to plan their grazing to mimic nature. This requires increasing camp numbers while decreasing their size, and grazing with high stocking densities for short periods of time.

Alternatively, in large camps, stock can be herded during the day in tight groups to achieve the same effect. Freshly grazed vegetation is given a period of time from 30 days to nine months to recover, depending on recovery rate, the environment and the overall management plan.

Allan points out that because of the way humans have been running livestock, grazing land is over-rested. "Over-resting destroys perennial grass species," he says. "This happens in many rotational grazing situations where animals are in big camps grazing or overgrazing plants in certain sections, while plants in other sections are over-rested by never being grazed. They become moribund and unproductive because there are no natural disturbances of the plants or the soil."

It has been an uphill battle for Allan to demonstrate the wisdom of what is now known as holistic farming, holistic range management or holistic veld management. Conventional agricultural thinking through the decades proposed the opposite. In South Africa, for example, the state introduced a stock reduction plan about 50 years ago on the basis that the major cause of veld deterioration and soil erosion was over-stocking.

The insight of men such as Allan Savory and South African vegetation specialist John Acocks, whose famous comment that the land was "understocked and overgrazed," was ignored by the government, conventional scientists and most farmers. A few independently minded farmers who understood the wisdom of what Allan and John were saying today present their farms as proof of what can be achieved with good holistic management. Good examples are the farms of the Jack family from Beaufort West and the Speedy family in Vryburg.

Both farmers met Allan in the 1960s and have been farming holistically since then. Jennifer Speedy, who attended the workshop, farms with her father Sandy. They run 1,556 Nguni cattle on their farm in 240 grazing camps of about 20ha [hectare] per camp. A one-day grazing period is alternated with a recovery period of 60 or more days. "Looking back 40 to 50 years later, I am convinced we took the right road although we made many mistakes. If I could relive my life I would choose the same road," says Sandy.

"We learnt the hard way about many things such as required grazing pressure, the timing of grazing and recovery, managing the herd and the grass to ensure that stock are in the right place on the farm at the right time of the year, keeping cow-calf pairs together in a relatively densely packed herd of breeding cows calving on the move, and supplying water to a large moving herd.

"It's been hard work, but the rewards have made it worthwhile. Our beef production has doubled and is set to double again. Our stocking rate has increased from about 6 ha/MLU [mature livestock unit] to 2.5 ha/MLU. The grass cover has become denser and the species composition of the sward is changing for the better."

Allan is convinced that, with greatly increased livestock numbers and holistic planned grazing, even deserts such as the Sahara in Africa or the Tihama in Yemen can be transformed.

Tracking their course, Sandy says that they have come a long way and adds that from where he stands now the potential seems unlimited. It is this kind of testimony that debunks Allan's detractors. "Make no mistake I have seen failures too, in stop-start operations all over the world, but when the grazing is well planned and sound holistic management is in place, it cannot fail," stresses Allan.

Land Restoration

Based in Boulder, Colorado, in the US, the Savory Institute plans to restore one billion acres (404 million hectares) of land by establishing 100 holistic agricultural hubs worldwide, 40 of which will be in Africa. "What I have to share are a few profound principles that can make a huge difference to people's lives, can yield 300% more profit than conventional approaches, and can provide an anchor for our planet in these times of climate change," explains Allan.

"Climate change is the most serious threat humanity has ever faced. A tsunami of global economic, social and environmental proportions is upon us and agriculture has a central role to play. At the moment agriculture is producing more eroding soil than food, but if we change our approach, livestock farmers will become the most important people in the world because of our capability of reversing desertification."

Allan is convinced that, with greatly increased livestock numbers and holistic planned grazing, even deserts such as the Sahara in Africa or the Tihama in Yemen can be transformed. In the campaign to halt desertification, scientists have been advising governments to stop nomadic pastoralism. Allan cites the example of the shooting of 50,000 Navaho sheep by the US government because of the belief that they were causing desertification.

"After the livestock were removed the desertification got worse. The same happened in Africa after mass game culling programmes. The livestock and game were not the problem, the problem was that there wasn't sufficient animal impact and hoof action, and the animals were too sedentary," he explains. "Early Scottish shepherds understood this and spoke of the 'golden hoof of the sheep.'

"Early South African writers observed and described the thundering hooves of migrating animals, healthy grasslands and reedbeds. That land with the same rainfall is now arid and desertifying. We need to hammer the land with mass hoof action; we need to stimulate litter build-up, which slows down water and soil run-off, evaporation and wind erosion. This encourages plant growth and increases plant cover. The seed stores are all there, waiting for the right environment to germinate, but they cannot germinate in compacted, capped soil," says Allan.

Many farmers believe that burning stimulates plant growth, but Allan points out the damage this causes. "Africa is burning more than 2 billion acres (809 million hectares) of grasslands a year, the immense carbon emission significantly contributing to climate change and destroying the soil. Soil is a living organism like skin, if you burn too much of it, it dies," he says.

"Dead soil cannot support healthy vegetation and each burn destroys the litter between the plants. Ultimately the space between plants gets greater and greater. This is the opposite of what we want to achieve because we need the plants to be close together to bind the soil and make the rainfall more effective. Too many scientists and farmers confuse 'total rainfall' with 'effective rainfall.' A farmer with a high total rainfall may have less effective rainfall than a farmer with a lower total rainfall, depending on how each manages his soil and vegetation."

The livestock graze as one large, undivided herd from dawn to sunset under the close supervision of full-time herders.

A fine example of what can be achieved with effective rainfall and the hoof action of cattle and game is to be found on the 2,630ha Dimbangombe Ranch in the Hwange communal lands near Victoria Falls, Zimbabwe, which has an annual but erratic rainfall of 600mm. The Africa Centre for Holistic Management, of which Allan is chairperson, manages the land in partnership with local chiefs.

"Ten years ago the veld was in a bad state. The best areas had been 90% bare for about 30 years because of continuous grazing and frequent burning," recalls Allan. Increasing livestock numbers by 400% (to 500 cattle and some goats) and following a programme of holistic planned grazing, veld degradation has been reversed, dead soil has been transformed into a thriving grassland, and rivers, streams and pools that had dried up now flow again.

The livestock graze as one large, undivided herd from dawn to sunset under the close supervision of full-time herders, who herd from the front to control the pace at which the animals move. The herd is never spread; it operates as a concentrated unit occupying less than a hectare at any given time, and moving constantly. Because the cattle graze, unfenced, on the same land as wildlife, they are herded into portable kraals at night.

"We achieve extremely high animal impact in the kraals and we use them for no more than seven consecutive nights to heal any seriously eroding gullies or extremely compacted bare soil," Allan explains. Fixed-point photography over several years has monitored the dramatic reversal of desertification at these sites. He advises anyone planning to farm holistically to take the official stocking rate for the area as a general stocking guideline, but to begin by doubling the rate.

"Start your planned grazing straight away and then build up from there. Take fixed point photos each season and you'll be amazed at the recovery of the veld and the animal numbers you can run on your farm after a few years."

Plant-Based Diets' Environmental Impact Examined in French Study

Andrew Seaman

Andrew Seaman is a reporter covering health and health-care policy for Reuters.

A nutritious diet that includes lots of fruits and vegetables might be healthier for humans but not necessarily healthier for the environment, according to a French study.

After analyzing the eating habits of about 2,000 French adults, and the greenhouse gas emissions generated by producing the plants, fish, meat, fowl and other ingredients, researchers concluded in *The American Journal of Clinical Nutrition* that such a diet might not be the greenest in environmental impact.

"When you eat healthy, you have to eat a lot of food that has a low content of energy. You have to eat a lot of fruits and vegetables," said Nicole Darmon, the study's senior author from the National Research Institute of Agronomy in Marseille, France.

The Source of Greenhouse Gases

Growing fruits and vegetables doesn't produce as much greenhouse gas as raising cattle or livestock, but food production—including the use of farming equipment and transportation—is estimated to be responsible for 15 percent to 30 percent of greenhouse gas emissions in development countries, the authors said.

Scientists have long advised people to switch to a plant-based diet to benefit the environment and their own health.

To more closely examine that premise, Darmon and her colleagues used food diaries from 1,918 French adults to compare the nutritional quality of people's real-world diets and how much greenhouse gas they produced.

From the diaries that were kept for seven days between 2006 and 2007, the researchers identified the 400 most commonly consumed foods. They then used a database to find out how much greenhouse gas was emitted to produce each one, measured as the grams of carbon dioxide equivalent per 100 grams of food.

All aspects of a food's lifecycle were taken into account, including how it was cooked, Darmon said.

"The only step that wasn't taken into account was the transport from the supermarket to the home," she added.

Overall, about 1,600 grams of carbon dioxide were emitted for every 100 grams of meat produced. That's more than 15 times the amount of greenhouse gas emitted during the production of fruits, vegetables and starches and about 2.5 times as much greenhouse gas as that from fish, pork, poultry and eggs.

Greens . . . ended up emitting more gas for the calories than starches, sweets, salty snacks, dairy and fats.

That gap narrowed, however, when the researchers looked at how many grams of carbon dioxide were emitted per 100 kilocalories (kcal)—a measure of energy in food.

The most greenhouse gas—857 grams—was still emitted to produce 100 kcal of meat, but only about three times the emissions from a comparable amount of energy from fruit and vegetables.

Greens also ended up emitting more gas for the calories than starches, sweets, salty snacks, dairy and fats. It was also about as much gas as pork, poultry and eggs.

When Darmon and her colleagues looked at what people actually ate to get a certain amount of energy from food every day, they found that the "highest-quality" diets in health terms—those high in fruit, vegetables and fish—were linked to about as much, if not more, greenhouse gas emissions as low-quality diets that were high in sweets and salts.

Overall, the documented diets were responsible for around 5,000 grams of greenhouse gas emissions per day per person.

Darmon said that's because people who eat a plant-based diet need to eat more produce to get the amount of energy they'd have in a piece of meat.

Roni Neff, the director of research and policy at Johns Hopkins Bloomberg School of Public Health's Center for a Livable Future, cautioned against taking the findings too literally. For example, according to the study's calculations, people would need to eat about four kilograms (nine pounds) of fruit and vegetables to make up for a smaller serving of meat.

"I think they're raising a lot of important questions that need further investigation," she said.

CHAPTER 2

What Are the Moral and Spiritual Implications of Vegetarianism?

Overview: Vegetarians' Beliefs Are Just as Sincere as Those of Traditional Religious Faiths

Sherry F. Colb

Sherry F. Colb is a regular columnist for the legal website Justia and a professor of law at Cornell Law School. She is also the author of Mind if I Order the Cheeseburger?: And Other Questions People Ask Vegans.

In December 2010, the Cincinnati Children's Hospital Medical Center fired Sakile S. Chenzira, a Customer Service Representative, for refusing to get a seasonal flu vaccination, in violation of the hospital's policy. Ms. Chenzira had refused the vaccine because she is a vegan, and the vaccine is produced in chicken's eggs, which are taken from animals and therefore are not vegan.

After being fired, Ms. Chenzira brought a lawsuit in federal court against the hospital, alleging—among other claims—that her termination violated her federal right under Title VII of the 1964 Civil Rights act to be free from religious discrimination. The defendant moved to dismiss the claim, arguing that veganism does not qualify as a religion that triggers the protection of the law.

In a move that some have found surprising, a federal district court in the Southern District of Ohio denied the defendant's motion to dismiss the case, concluding that a vegan may, depending on the evidence, have a legal ground for claiming that her veganism qualifies for the same protection as a sincerely held religious belief. In this column, I will examine the district judge's decision and explain what it does and does not say about the plaintiff's decision to refuse a flu vaccine.

What Is a Vegan?

To have an informed discussion of whether a vegan is sufficiently comparable to a practitioner of Christianity or Islam to trigger the protection of a law prohibiting religious discrimination, it is important first to understand what it means to be a vegan. Like practitioners of traditional religions, vegans have diverse ways of living and of manifesting their commitment to veganism. Most ethical vegans do, however, share a commitment to the proposition that it is wrong to inflict suffering and death on animals in order to meet needs that can be met in other ways.

When health or safety is at risk and alternatives are unavailable, some people who consider themselves ethical vegans will take a non-vegan medicine, while others will not.

More concretely, this means that ethical vegans choose (a) to consume a plant-based diet, avoiding the flesh and bodily secretions (such as milk and eggs) of nonhuman animals, including cows, chickens, and fishes; (2) to wear exclusively non-animal-based clothing in lieu of fur, leather, wool, and other materials derived from the exploitation (and virtually always the slaughter, when animals outlive their utility to humans) of animals; and (c) to use body care products, such as shampoo, soap, and deodorants, that are derived from non-animal sources and that were safety-tested without the use of animals.

On the question of medications and vaccines, ethical vegans take different positions, and most acknowledge that the issue is far more difficult than the question whether to buy chickens' eggs or cows' milk yogurt at the supermarket. Though the vaccine is not a vegan product, some vegans might take the view that in the absence of a vegan alternative vaccination, the existing flu shot is necessary to the vegan's own or to others' health.

For similar reasons, a vegan who is sick and needs a medication that is currently available only in a form that contains animal ingredients might conclude that necessity permits the use of the medication. At the present time, U.S. law also requires that all medications in the United States be tested on animals, and many are synthesized with non-vegan additives, so vegans often lack the option of taking a vegan version of the medicine. When health or safety is at risk and alternatives are unavailable, some people who consider themselves ethical vegans will take a non-vegan medicine, while others will not.

What Is a Religion?

The next question to confront, in determining whether veganism qualifies as a religion under Title VII, is this one: What is a religion? Some religions are old and thus long-recognized as religions, including the well-known families of religion that go under the headings of Buddhism, Hinduism, Judaism, Christianity, and Islam. A member of one of these faiths may encounter little resistance in claiming, in an anti-discrimination legal action, that he or she is a member of a religious group.

Under the Code of Federal Regulations relevant to the definition of religion under federal anti-discrimination law, "[i]n most cases whether or not a practice or belief is religious is not at issue. However, in those cases in which the issue does exist, the [Equal Employment Opportunity] Commission will define religious practices to include moral or ethical beliefs as to what is right and wrong which are sincerely held with the strength of traditional religious views."

Though readers may associate religion with a belief in God, a person can in fact be a very committed practitioner of a religion without actually believing in any supernatural beings. Indeed, some established religions—such as Buddhism—do not necessarily even entail belief in such a being at all. Growing up as an Orthodox Jew, I learned that my religion did not require a belief in God or in any other phenomena; it required only that one conform one's behavior to religious requirements.

Ethical vegans . . . consider it wrongful for a person to participate in harming and slaughtering animals by consuming them or their hair, skin, or bodily secretions.

Is Veganism a Religion?

Using the criterion articulated above, and repeated by the district court in Ms. Chenzira's case, it is clear that ethical vegans do sincerely hold "moral or ethical beliefs as to what is right and wrong . . . with the strength of traditional religious views." To be sure, not everyone who identifies herself as a vegan necessarily holds the equivalent of a religious faith. Former President Bill Clinton, for example, has stopped eating animal-derived ingredients and has even described himself as a vegan. He apparently eats the way he does because he has discovered, through research and consultation with medical experts, that a whole-food, plant-based diet low in fat not only slows, but can actually reverse heart disease.

I was delighted to learn that Bill Clinton has chosen to eat in this way (and I hope that his wife, former Secretary of State Hilary Clinton, joins him in this healthful approach to eating). President Clinton's choice, however, does not seem to be connected to conscience or to a moral or ethical commitment. He wishes to eat healthful food, but he does not appear to believe (and has not, to my knowledge, stated) that it is unethical to consume flesh, secretions, or other products of animal agriculture. Instead, he apparently avoids doing so for health reasons, much as many people go to the gym to exercise for health reasons. And it would be far-fetched to claim that working out several days a week to stay healthy and fit is relevantly comparable to the practice of a religion.

Ethical vegans, by contrast, consider it wrongful for a person to participate in harming and slaughtering animals by consuming them or their hair, skin, or bodily secretions, even when doing so would pose no threat to the consumer's own health. Ethical vegans do not, moreover, generally consider it "wrong for me, but fine for you" to consume animal ingredients, in the way that consuming gluten or peanuts may be fine for me but highly undesirable for someone who suffers from celiac disease or peanut allergies, respectively.

Just as most of us consider it wrong for *anyone* to molest a child or to throw rocks at a puppy, vegans consider it wrong for anyone to consume cheese derived from a cow's breast milk or to consume a slaughtered chicken's flesh. Stated differently, vegans, like members of religious faiths more generally, are moral realists. We believe that some actions—such as participating in violence against defenseless human *and* nonhuman animals—are wrong. That is one of the reasons that many ethical vegans serve our houseguests only vegan food in our homes, regardless of what the guests might ordinarily select when eating by themselves.

Ethical veganism, by contrast to many religions, dictates no position on supernatural beings or events, one way or the other. Some vegans are members of a conventional, God-centered religious faith and share that belief system, while others consider themselves to be agnostics or atheists. Nonetheless, an ethical vegan's commitment to refusing flesh and animal secretions is often just as strong and sincere as a religious Jew's commitment to avoiding leavened bread during the Passover holiday or a religious Muslim's commitment to avoiding the flesh of pigs.

Vegetarianism Is a Moral Decision with Many Benefits

Melanie Joy

Melanie Joy is a psychologist, professor, and the author of numerous articles on psychology, animal protection, and social justice, as well as the book Why We Love Dogs, Eat Pigs, and Wear Cows. *She is also the founder and president of the Carnism Awareness and Action Network.*

> As a medical doctor, once only interested in my patient's welfare, I was slow to see the bigger picture. I now understand that we must also consider our impact on the animals and the environment. Fortunately, these are not mutually exclusive goals.
>
> —*John McDougall, M.D.*

Many people embark on the journey of following a whole-food, plant-based diet with the sole intention of improving their heath and enhancing their quality of life. And while improved physical wellbeing is a worthy goal in-and-of itself and its benefits are indisputable, it is by no means the only benefit of eating "plant-strong." We cannot reduce eating to nothing more than what we put in our bodies any more than we can reduce foods to nothing more than their chemical properties (a whole apple, for instance, is not simply an aggregate of fiber, calories, and vitamins). Whether intentional or not, following a whole-food, plant-based diet is about much more than simply what we do—or do not—eat, and it therefore impacts much more than simply our physical health.

Following a whole-food, plant-based diet is about having the courage to step outside of the mainstream, animal-eating culture, a culture that seeks to keep us intellectually anesthetized and comfortably numb. (For more information on the mentality of the animal-eating culture, which I refer to as *carnism*, see carnism.com).

It is about reclaiming our health and redefining the very meaning and nature of eating and food. It is about being open to ideas that challenge the myths of the dominant culture in which we have all been indoctrinated—to critically examine longstanding "truths" that have been drummed into us by our parents, teachers, doctors, and society. It is about questioning the authorities we have learned to place our trust in and thus questioning our own relationship with authority and truth. It is about resisting the pressure to conform to a seductive yet destructive status quo and having the strength to hold onto our convictions in the face of deep-seated resistance to our lifestyle. (How often have you thrown up your hands in perplexed exasperation when, for instance, your dangerously overweight loved one, who's undergone triple bypass surgery, calls you crazy for suggesting they reduce their meat consumption? How often have you felt alienated at meals where otherwise conscientious, rational people cannot seem to remember or figure out how to prepare a plant-based meal so that you don't have to starve?) Following a whole-food, plant-based diet is about saying *yes* to *health, life,* and *truth*—and therefore saying *no* to the beliefs and behaviors of the dominant, animal-eating culture.

When We Say *Yes,* We Also Say *No* to Harm, Death, and Denial

When we say *yes* to *health*, we say *no* to *harm*. We protect our bodies as well of the bodies of the animals—approximately 20,000 of them per *minute* in the U.S. alone—who are brutally raised and slaughtered for their flesh and excretions. These beings exist in conditions that would horrify even the most thick-skinned of us. For instance, farmed animals are routinely castrated, de-beaked, and de-horned without any painkiller whatsoever. (The screams of piglets as their testicles are being crushed have literally traumatized animal advocates who must witness such procedures.) They are born and raised in crowded, filthy, dark environments where their existence is one of abject misery and terror. The females may be hooked up to "rape racks" where they are forcibly impregnated, over and over, only to have their offspring taken from them just hours after birth. (The wailing of cows whose babies have been dragged away is as haunting as the screams of piglets). They are shackled by their ankles, dragged along a conveyor belt, sliced open, and plunged into boiling water, often while fully conscious. Indeed, when we say *yes* to health and *no* to harm, we also say *yes* to *compassion* and *no* to *cruelty*. (And, as a bonus—since according to the United Nations animal agriculture is the leading cause of some of the most serious environmental problems in the world today, and according to Human Rights Watch conditions in U.S. meatpacking plants are so appalling they violate basic human rights—when we follow a whole food, plant-based diet we also say *no* to harming the environment and workers.)

When we say *yes* to *life*, we say *no* to *death*. We enhance our own life, but we also enhance other life: wildlife that is decimated by deforestation (according to the World Bank, approximately 91 percent of clear-cutting in the Brazilian rainforest is for cattle ranching); aquatic life—including unintentionally targeted species, or "bycatch," such as dolphins—that, according to the FAO [Food and Agriculture Organization of the United Nations], is exterminated by about 27 *million tons* per year by commercial fishing; plant life that is destroyed by vast quantities of toxic wastes dumped into the environment by CAFOs [concentrated animal feeding operations] ("factory farms"); and, of course, farmed animals. We enhance the life of pigs, chickens, fish, cows, and other sentient beings who, like all beings, have lives that matter to them and whom animal agriculture reduces to mere units of production. Indeed, when we say *yes* to life and *no* to death, we also say *yes* to *justice* and *no* to *oppression*. We no longer support *any unnecessary*—unjust—killing, including killing that is carried out on small-scale "humane" farms. While most people would, for example, recognize the injustice of killing a perfectly healthy golden retriever simply because they like the way her thighs taste, these same people nevertheless typically support the killing of other species under the very same circumstances. Following a whole-food, plant-based diet means saying *no* to the massive injustice that is animal agriculture, in all its permutations.

And finally, when we say *yes* to *truth*, we say *no* to *denial*. We no longer buy into the cultural fictions that deny the damage done by animal agriculture, and we recognize the Three Ns of Justification—eating animals is *normal, natural,* and *necessary*—as the myths that they are. We can also recognize that farmed animals are beings rather than objects, individuals rather than abstractions, and sentient species that are equally inedible (if we wouldn't eat a kitten, why eat a lamb?). When we remove the blinders of denial we see the truth—the truth that, when it comes to eating other living beings, we have been taught to numb ourselves, psychologically and emotionally. We have been taught to block our awareness and empathy so that we see corpses as cuisine and act accordingly. When we say *yes* to truth, we are more in alignment with our core values, values such as justice, reciprocity (the Golden Rule), and compassion. We are therefore more psychologically and ethically integrated, and we bring greater authenticity and integrity to our lives. And we can sleep better at night—not only because we are not polluting our bodies, but also because we are not polluting our hearts and minds.

When we follow a whole-food, plant-based diet, we inevitably become conscientious objectors to the oppressive, animal-eating culture. Eating—and not eating—animals is not a morally neutral act. By choosing to eat plants rather than animals we are making a statement and taking a stand. We are voting with our forks, and we are voting for far more than simply what we eat.

Vegetarianism Is the Only Morally Acceptable Diet

Robert Grillo

Robert Grillo is the founder and director of Free from Harm, a nonprofit animal rescue, education, and advocacy organization.

How many times have you heard someone justify their behavior based on the illogical premise that history somehow makes it *right* and assures its ethical legitimacy into the future? In fact, throughout history influential leaders and thinkers have used this same troubled logic to defend slavery, genocide, the oppression of women, racism, and discrimination based on a whole host of irrelevant criteria including sexual orientation, religion, color and now species.

In my discussions with people both online and in person, I find this interpretation of history and evolution to be one of the most common "apologies" for meat eating I hear these days. I see it as yet another way to avoid honestly confronting the moral issue of using and killing animals for food in an age when it is not necessary. Some actually sympathize with the position of vegans and vegetarians, yet still default to this argument which explains perhaps why 95% of us continue to blindly follow the cultural norms reinforced in us since childhood.

Modern Myths

But when we are open to taking a critical look at what we have been taught, the modern myth of humans evolving to eat meat can be challenged on several levels. Here are a few of them:

1. Because we are highly evolved moral beings, averse to violence and suffering.

If evolution teaches us anything at all, it teaches us that our moral consciousness and our emotional intelligence are a result of highly developed areas of our brain that afford us these faculties. ". . . Humans are the only animals that can intentionally structure the patterns of our lives according to a basic set of self-aware moral ideals," writes journalist and history professor James McWilliams. "This ability, which is generally premised on reducing unnecessary pain and suffering, happens to be the foundation of human civilization."

2. Because Einstein said so.

Ironically the idea that humans have somehow evolved to eat meat stands in stark contrast to the evolutionary and ethical theory of one of the greatest scientific minds who ever lived, Albert Einstein. Einstein argued that humankind would need to evolve to vegetarianism to essentially save himself and the planet. "Nothing will benefit human health and increase the chances for survival of life on earth as much as the evolution to a vegetarian diet."

No one is arguing that we don't have a long history of hunting and eating animals. The more timely question is why . . . would we want to focus on what our ancestors ate some 10,000 or more years ago?

So if the argument favoring history carries so much weight for most of us, will a mainstream move to vegetarianism as Einstein predicted ever occur? I think so. For one thing, the interpretation of history that meat eaters use to justify meat eating is selectively referenced from those historical sources that support the practice of meat-eating, while ignoring the rest of our history—namely our close ancestral relatives who were primarily or entirely herbivores.

3. Because so-called progressives should think progressively about animals too.

Even more ironic still is how otherwise progressive-minded people today continue to support the oppressive forces in our society with their eating habits, the same forces that they have adamantly opposed in other areas of their life—in their political leanings, in their religious and spiritual beliefs, in the kind of media and entertainment they seek, in the sort of books and magazines they read, etc. Still the oppression of animals remains unexamined for most progressives, and their diets reveal a deep denial of this oppression. But even this recalcitrance appears to be softening. Victoria Moran, author of *Main Street Vegan*, recounts that at one point her friend Michael Moore was "anti-vegan" but is now on the vegan path.

4. Because glorifying the history of humankind's baser instincts thwarts evolution.

Yet even in the face of these exciting new developments, groups like the Weston A. Price Foundation argue that evolution essentially has a gun to our heads to consume animal products (Horn, *Meat Logic*). Other variations on the "we've always eaten animals" logic include the popular Paleo diet, whose fan sites unearth a vast ancestral mythology on the rituals of eating animals, referencing allegedly scientific, anthropological and cultural studies to prove it. Prehistoric humans and their ancestors ate some amount of meat. There's no question about that. However, an in-depth analysis by science writer Rob Dunn published in the *Scientific American* reports on recent studies indicating that "Human Ancestors Were Nearly All Vegetarians." But, again, is what our ancestors ate really relevant to the very different circumstances we face today regarding our food choices and lifestyles? We are no more compelled to eat like our ancestors than we are to practice cannibalism, rape, slavery, murder, or any of the other violent traditions which are all an unfortunate part of our human legacy.

5. Because by focusing on our potential to do good now, we overcome the oppressive tendencies of our past.

All this talk of what is right for us to eat based on past examples distracts us from dealing with the here and now, over which we have complete control. No one is arguing that we don't have a long history of hunting and eating animals. The more timely question is why, in an age when meat eating is unnecessary (for the vast majority of the human population), would we want to focus on what our ancestors ate some 10,000 or more years ago? To paraphrase author Colleen Patrick Goudreau, why would we want to base our ethics for eating on our paleontological ancestors whose lives were dictated by a vastly different set of circumstances and about whom we still have many unanswered questions? Certainly there are lessons to learn from history on many levels, but in relating historical facts to present circumstances, context and relevancy are everything.

> Our deplorable and largely unchallenged legacy of treating animals as property, currency, objects and cheap, disposable pieces of meat is coming under greater scrutiny than ever before in our history.

6. Because the lessons from history strongly support the opposite.

When confronting the person who argues his case based on history, I say, first, agree with that arguer wholeheartedly. Then explain how the history and evolution of other social justice movements can instruct and galvanize us regarding the future of the vegan/animal rights movement. One common thread that runs through all of these movements is that they were ultimately successful in permeating mainstream culture and society.

They may have begun as *fringe* movements whose followers were ridiculed and dismissed as *extremists*, but their leaders ended up being canonized in the history books and described as pioneers who popularized their social movements. And many of these leaders clearly articulated the need for both human and non human animal rights, including Cezar Chavez, Martin Luther King Jr., and Alice Walker. Filmmaker and activist James LaVeck makes a compelling case for how the British anti-slavery movement serves as an example and inspiration for the contemporary animal rights movement in his presentation, "Let's Not Give Up Before We Get Started."

7. Because our appetite for justice is far stronger.

In the words of Victor Hugo, "There is nothing more powerful than an idea whose time has come." It appears that we are standing on the threshold of an era when the tyranny of history is about to be dealt yet another serious blow. As the vegan/animal rights movement continues to gain momentum, our deplorable and largely unchallenged legacy of treating animals as property, currency, objects and cheap, disposable pieces of meat is coming under greater scrutiny than ever before in our history. This makes the infamous statement, "*man has evolved to eat meat*," seem even more hopelessly out-of-touch and reactionary, revealing an attitude that clings desperately to the past and fears change, even when that change promises to reconnect us with the most fundamental and universal principle of justice and respect for all. I believe justice will ultimately prevail in the end.

Buddhists Are Permitted to Consume Meat

Wayne Hughes

Wayne Hughes is an ordained cleric in the Order of Pragmatic Buddhists and leader of the St. Louis chapter of the Center for Pragmatic Buddhists.

The season of charcoal being fired up in the grill is nearly on us. Tasty burgers, tender zucchinis, rich steaks, sweet red peppers, plump hot dogs, crunchy asparagus, barbequed pork steaks, slices of juicy pineapple . . . just to mention some . . . will soon add their delicious aromas to the smoky air. What is a Buddhist to do?

"But the idea that Buddhists have always been, and always should be, vegetarians is pure myth." Stephen Asma, *Why I am a Buddhist: No Nonsense Buddhism with Red Meat and Whiskey.*

One of the most frequently asked questions about being a Buddhist is, "Do I have to be a vegetarian to be a Buddhist?" The answer is no. Though opinions and scholarship differ depending on Buddhist tradition or personal preference, in the end it doesn't really matter whether, like some Mahayanists strongly believe the Buddha was a vegetarian or not. In the Mahaparnibbana Sutta the dish that the Buddha was served prior to his death was called sukara-maddava (soft pork) and there are differences of opinion whether it was actually pork or a dish of something associated with pigs, mushrooms being one translation put forth. Consider hot dogs. There is no dog in them. This may be the case with sukkara-muddava, no pork in it. Here again, does it really matter?

The Three Pure Precepts

This inevitably brings up the next question, "What about the Three Pure Precepts: cease to do harm, do only good, do good for others?" While later Mahayanist texts like Lankavatara Sutra strongly favor a vegetarian diet it came about through cultural changes as Buddhist monks began to gather in fixed location monasteries and monks no longer performed alms rounds. Before that the Buddha instructed all monks to wander, to visit the towns and villages, to accept the alms they were given, to teach and to [offer] examples to others. Once the monastics spent the majority of their time in monasteries the local lay people began [to be] responsible for supporting them. This meant that any meats were most likely killed and butchered by the lay people specifically for the monastic community, one of the Five Instances to be avoided in the consumption of meat that the Buddha explains in the Jivaka Sutta. Zen Master D.T. Suzuki in his commentary on the Lankavatara Sutta states that the chapter dealing with eating meat was added in later versions of the sutta and was likely not the authentic words of the Buddha. There is ample evidence in the Pali Nikayas that show that this total rejection of meat as part of the diet was not part of early Buddhist philosophy.

In the Jivaka Sutta (Majjhima Nikaya, #55) the Awakened One answers Jivaka's questions about the consumption of meat:

"Thus I have heard:"

"Jivaka, who ever destroys living things on account of the Awakened One or the disciples of the Awakened One, accumulate much demerit on five instances: If he said, go bring that living thing of such name. In this first instance he accumulates much demerit. If that living thing is pulled along, tied, with pain at the throat, feeling displeased and unpleasant. In this second instance he accumulates much demerit. If it was said, go kill that animal. In this third instance he accumulates much demerit. When killing if that animal feels displeased and unpleasant, in this fourth instance he accumulates much demerit. When the Awakened One or a disciple tastes that unsuitable food. In this fifth instance he accumulates much demerit. Jivaka, if anyone destroys the life of a living thing on account of the Awakened One or a disciple of the Awakened One, he accumulates much demerit on these five instances."

If one wants to make a case for their own choice of vegetarianism it should be from the platform of loving-kindness and equanimity, not from a misguided idea that the "Buddha said so."

The five instances the Buddha speaks of are: 1) if a specific living thing is requested, 2) if the living thing is being mistreated or mishandled, 3) if the intent was the animal was killed directly for the consumption of the monk, 4) if the living thing is nervous or frightened, 5) if knowing any of these things have happened and the person eats the meat anyway. In any of these instances either the consumer, the provider, or both will accumulate demerits. Pragmatically speaking the word demerit is a placeholder for the concept of engendering negative karma. By participating in a negative act there will be negative consequences that we may, or may not realize ourselves. A simple example would be that because the abuse of one animal is accepted then the door is open for the same to happen to others.

This sutta offers that if one wants to make a case for their own choice of vegetarianism it should be from the platform of loving-kindness and equanimity, not from a misguided idea that the "Buddha said so." Remember it is also about psycho-emotional suffering or unsatisfactoriness that eating meat might cause you as well as the harm being done to other creatures.

Cease to Do Harm

The first Pure Precept directs us to "cease to do harm," to refrain from unintentional acts of killing whenever possible. Eating meat is not considered an instance of killing as long as two basic rules are followed: the animal is not tortured or made to suffer, and the meat was not specifically butchered for the monk with their knowledge. So, the issue is causing unneeded pain to animals. It is important to keep in mind that this admonition was for monastics though it can be viewed as a guide to the devout lay person also.

As it is unseemly for a Buddhist monk to make special food requests they would have to make a simple choice: eat or starve.

Isn't the meat we get at the grocery store or local Farmer's Market killed for us "by proxy"? There is little we consume that hasn't entailed "killing by proxy," from the electricity we use, the houses we live in, and the clothes we wear. Buddhist scriptures and books are written on paper whose manufacture resulted in the destruction of animal habitat. There are insects, rodents and other critters killed to produce even a vegetarian diet. It is impossible for us to separate ourselves from the reality of the Universe we live in. What we can do is be mindful of where our sustenance comes from and let that guide our intent and limit our consumption.

To better understand this "Middle Path" to the eating of meat we have to look to history as well as intent. In Siddhartha's time and culture there were no 'Buddhists' but there were holy men, seers and mendicants of all types, including followers of the Awakened One who subsisted off the generosity of the people. Lay people offered food out of respect without considering the strictures of the receiver. When meat was offered the monk accepted it graciously and ate it. To reject such an offer would have caused suffering in the person offering it and deprive the lay person of performing a selfless act, one that gain them merit in this life.

Buddhists all over the world eat meat. In some parts of the world it is common for meals to be cooked in a broth made from meat or fish. As it is unseemly for a Buddhist monk to make special food requests they would have to make a simple choice: eat or starve.

You may have seen or heard the stories of Tibetan monks sifting through dirt to save worms and bugs from being harmed during the building of a temple. Some of those same monks regularly have meat as part of their diet. This may seem contradictory but what it is is situational. There is a need for the human body to have protein, there is a need for the lay person to garner merit in the Tibetan culture, but there isn't a need to cause unnecessary suffering to living beings. The monks and lay people certainly don't save every worm and bug but they do what they can, their intention is good and the effort is one that builds merit in their Buddhist culture.

In our own time and culture there are Buddhists, and those of other worldviews who are smug vegetarians likely to judge others for eating meat. In contemporary Theravadan view a monk or lay person who claims spiritual superiority because they are a vegetarian is considered to have an immature practice, one where the ego is still prevalent.

A Choice, Not a Commandment

In the Frequently Asked Questions section of the Accesstoinsight website in answer to the question: "Do Buddhists have to be vegetarian?", they answer that the choice of whether or not to eat meat is a personal choice in Theravadan Buddhism. Though many who choose to follow the Middle Path may eventually decline to eat meat out of compassion for animals, vegetarianism is a choice not a commandment.

This is a complicated issue whether one is a Buddhist or not. Buddhist philosophy doesn't demand that one be a vegetarian but it does offer us ways to make that decision on our own.

Whichever we choose, herbivore or carnivore or omnivore, we must remain mindful of our interconnection with everything around us. As part of our daily practice we must develop an awareness of those connections and what we eat can be an opportunity to practice. Before each meal take a moment to respect the journey what you are about to eat took to get to you.

> "Let us be mindful of the journey this food took to reach us. May the energy we derive from consuming it be used to promote human flourishing."

There Are Spiritual Benefits to Vegetarianism

George Burke

George Burke (Swami Nirmalananda Giri) is the founder and director of the Light of the Spirit Monastery in Cedar Crest, New Mexico.

Bondage and liberation are states of mind. The mind, as a mass of vibrating energy, is limited by the constitution or condition of that energy. If the energy is heavy or inert, little can be done with it to produce the state of silence and clarity needed to reflect the truth of spirit. Certain elements darken the mind and make it thick or heavy, vibrating very slowly—sometimes seemingly not at all. On the other hand, some elements lighten the mind, making it fluid and subtle, vibrating at a very high level. It is this latter condition that is needed for attaining the state of liberation—or rather, the state that liberates the spirit from the illusion of bondage and suffering. It is really the mind that becomes liberated, but that liberation also affects the essentially ever-free spirit and sets it free. To attain such liberation the mind must be purified and refined, vegetarian diet being one of the best and strongest means for its purification.

Diet and Consciousness

Although diet is commonly considered a matter of physical health alone, since the Hermetic principle "as above, so below" is a fundamental truth of the cosmos, diet is a crucial aspect of emotional, intellectual, and spiritual development. For diet and consciousness are interrelated, and purity of diet is an effective aid to purity and clarity of consciousness.

The purification of our subtler levels depends upon the purification of our physical entity. This makes sense when we realize that all that goes to constitute a human being is formed of energies of various types, and the only source of energy is that which is brought into the body through sunlight, air, and food. And it is material food that provides by far the greatest amount of the energy from which our multilevel complex is shaped.

When we realize that any physical object has all the levels which we do, namely, the physical, biomagnetic, sensory, intellectual and will bodies, we can understand the importance of the kind and quality of food we eat. For not only does the physical substance of the food become assimilated into our physical body, so also do the subtler energies become united to our inner levels. This is the teaching of the Chandogya Upanishad: "Mind consists of food. That which is the subtle part of milk moves upward when the milk is churned and becomes butter. In the same manner, the subtle part of the food that is eaten moves upward and becomes mind. Thus, mind consists of food."

We cannot get a marble statue from clay, nor can we get wheat bread from barley meal—the end product is still going to consist of the nature of the material started with. So it is with all our bodies, gross and subtle. They will reflect the character of the food which has gone into their formation.

First we get these energy levels from our parents, but as we grow and develop we replace and increase those energies through the food we eat.

Nothing that exists is "solid matter." All physical objects are formed of molecules that are formed of atoms that are formed of particles that in the ultimate analysis are vibrating energy—not "things" at all. The only difference between gold, wood, water, and living human flesh is the pattern or behavior of the energy of which they are composed. If we go through the whole range of relative existence from the bottom—where we are—right up to the top, to (but not including) the realm of pure spirit, it is all energy of varying kinds, though one in essence.

The same is true of our individual, private universe we call "me." It is composed of successive layers of energy from very subtle to very gross. All the levels of energy that exist in creation exist in us as well. We are actually small reflections of the greater universe. Our spirit pervades our little cosmos, enlivening and directing it, just as God pervades, enlivens, and directs the universe.

All which we experience as "us" are just different strata of cosmic energy vibrating at differing rates. The physical body is the densest stratum, behind which is the stratum of biomagnetic energy that keeps the body going and links it to another field of energy which is the mind. (By "mind" is meant the percepting part of us which can see, hear, smell and so on, by means of the messages conveyed from the sense organs through the nervous system into the brain.) Beyond the mind is the intellect, the part of us that not only sees a hand but knows it is a hand—and not a foot. Beyond the intellect is an even subtler level from which our power of will arises. Human consciousness and human behavior are nothing but the states and activities of these various bodies of vibrating energy.

From whence do all these energy layers come? First we get these energy levels from our parents, but as we grow and develop we replace and increase those energies through the food we eat, although we receive some energy from light and air.

We Are What We Eat

It is obvious, then, that the food we eat is going to determine the quality and condition of all the levels of our being. Our food has the same levels we do, and the different energies of the food are absorbed into our corresponding levels. Therefore when we eat something, it not only affects us on all levels of our existence, it becomes those levels. In this very real sense we indeed are what we eat. In esoteric philosophy our various levels are looked upon as separate bodies through which our consciousness operates. Since those bodies are formed essentially from the food we eat, they will be conditioned by and function according to the kind of energy extracted from the food. We are very much like the child's toy that is a series of colored rings stacked on a rod. That is, we are successive layers of subtler and subtler energy that are connected to the physical body. From these energy levels the different life processes are empowered and administered.

If we take the energies of plants into our higher levels we will then naturally develop intuition and other subtle perceptions.

When the energies within us are positive, they produce harmonious states of mind and behavior. But when the energies are negative, they move in a random and chaotic manner and produce negative states of mind and, consequently, negative behavior. Moreover, these toxic energies can also manifest as physical illnesses or defects. Substances that are toxic to the body—such as meat, alcohol, nicotine, and drugs—are toxic on the inner levels as well, and their ingestion poisons all our bodies by putting into them negative energies which are going to manifest in the disrupting manner just described. On the other hand, fruits, vegetables, and grains are reservoirs of pure, basic life energies which are very light and malleable. These energies are easily assimilated into all our bodies and made to take on our specific, unique life vibrations and karmic patterns.

As stated at the very beginning, the bondage and liberation of an individual is exclusively a matter of his mind, and the process of liberation is a matter of purifying and transmuting the mind. Since the mind is formed of the subtle energies of that which we eat, we can realize that diet is one of the most crucial aspects of the spiritual aspirant's regimen, for it will determine the quality and effectiveness of his meditation experience. Just as soft wax readily takes the impression of a stamp and retains it—in contrast to cold, hard wax—so the mind formed of light and pure food energies will respond most readily and permanently to the liberating samskaras produced by meditation. Diet, then, can be a major determinant of our success or failure in spiritual life.

What is perception? Volumes have been written on that question, but we can consider it very simply. The mind is a field of energy which, when acted upon, is modified. Those modifications are the perceptions which the pure consciousness of the spirit witnesses, and which the intellect—also an energy field—classifies and evaluates. So the mind shapes itself in response to stimuli, and it is the modifications of the mind-energy which we perceive—not the actual thing itself. Obviously, then, the mind should be extremely sensitive and capable of easily forming into the patterns of perception. For this to be so, the mind (and intellectual) energies must be light and fluid. Such energies are obtained through eating substances composed of those energies—and those substances are fruits, vegetables, and grains.

It has been scientifically proven that plants react to thoughts—they are telepathic. If we take the energies of plants into our higher levels we will then naturally develop intuition and other subtle perceptions.

To help us better understand the mechanics of developing higher consciousness, we can consider the behavior of water. A bowl of water can easily be made to form into waves and eddies in response to movements of the bowl or of air currents. Thick syrup, on the other hand, will respond very little, and tar will not respond at all. So it is with the mind according to the type of energies which go into its composition.

For the intentional evolution of consciousness, the mind has to be very light and responsive, and that is accomplished mostly through diet. The mind must not only be sensitive to random impressions, it must also be shaped by our illumined wills. In a sense, we must sculpt our minds, forming them into instruments of higher awareness. To facilitate this, the mind must be as malleable as possible.

Purification and repositioning is not possible with energies other than those absorbed from sunlight, air, and plant life.

Just as cold clay cannot be worked with for modeling, but warm clay is easily used, in the same way the mind must be responsive to shaping by our will. Animal energies were never meant for higher consciousness, and consequently cannot be attuned to anything beyond the most mundane perceptions. The energies of fruits, vegetables, and grains, being unconditioned, can easily be made to vibrate to the highest potential.

The Spiritual Value of Vegetarianism

The major thing to keep in mind when considering the subject of vegetarianism is its relevancy in relation to our explorations of consciousness. We need only ask: Does it facilitate my spiritual growth—the development and expansion of my consciousness? The answer is Yes.

"One acts according to one's prakriti. Even the jnani does so. Beings follow their own prakriti; what will restraint accomplish?" (Bhagavad Gita 3:33). Many supposedly moral or spiritual problems are only matters of energy behavior. If the energies are purified and re-centered where they belong, instantly the problem vanishes. But such a purification and repositioning is not possible with energies other than those absorbed from sunlight, air, and plant life.

Practices for conscious evolution consist of two processes: (1) purification, refinement, and repolarization of energies and (2) placement of energies in higher levels. This means that our energies must be responsive, malleable and moveable.

Appollonius of Tyana, a great Master who lived in Greece shortly before the time of Jesus, was asked how he was able to work miracles. His simple answer was: "I have never eaten the flesh of animals." Of course he did not mean that abstinence from meat alone made him a miracle-worker—otherwise all vegetarian animals and humans would work miracles naturally. What he meant was that the condition of his mind and body, resulting from being a strict vegetarian, had enabled him to successfully engage in the inner disciplines required for spiritual enlightenment—disciplines he had learned from the yogis of India.

The best part about all this is that you can discover the truth for yourself by simply trying a vegetarian diet. Of course it must be a sensible one with those things that will nourish the body correctly. But you need only go on a vegetarian diet, eat correctly, and watch for the benefit. It will come.

There Is a Moral Middle Ground in the Omnivore vs. Vegetarian Debate

Joe Perez

Joe Perez is a spiritual mentor, author, poet, and scholar and the associate director and scholar-in-residence at the Center for World Spirituality.

Although I have felt guilty since childhood for eating animals, I have not succeeded in the past at becoming vegetarian and probably will never totally give up meat or dairy products. The moral case against eating meat is strong, but that doesn't mean I have found the arguments in favor of strict vegetarianism convincing.

I was raised with a stereotypical American diet in which meat is served in nearly every meal. But I have evolved to find for myself a stance which is less absolute than Vegetarian v. Carnivore, and done so by examining my actions from a worldcentric perspective.

The bottom line is that I have gradually found myself eating significantly less meat as a personal matter and choosing meats which are farmed humanely. I have rejected approaches to diet based on mere personal preference or ideology. Instead, I've chosen an ethos of meat on a middle path, one which would please neither vegetarians nor carnivores.

As I see it, a dietary philosophy which bans meat and brands opponents as murderers or one which reduces animals to objects for domination are unnecessarily extreme. Instead, an Integral vision asks us to consider animals as worthy of respect as our co-inhabitants of the Earth with intrinsic value, but it stops short of viewing their consumption as an intrinsic evil. We are asked to maximize our compassion for animal life as an integral part of the spiral of evolution and to weigh the costs and benefits of our relationship to animals.

The Costs of a Meat-Based Diet

The costs of a meat-based diet are projected to get worse in the years ahead. According to a 2012 report on Climate Central by John Vidal of *The Guardian*, leading water scientists have warned us that food shortages will become catastrophic over the next 40 years unless the world's population switches almost completely to a vegetarian diet. Already hunger or malnourishment are a fact of life for 2 billion people, and the water and food shortages ahead will grow much worse if meat eating continues on its current trajectory.

When we take a worldcentric perspective—for instance, trying to weigh the needs of the planet as a whole in our individual decision-making—we may ask: How much would the world need to change? The leading water scientists say that humans currently derive 20 percent of their protein from animal-based products right now, but this may need to drop to just 5 percent to feed the larger world population which will be alive by 2050.

With conscious eating choices, we are impacting other sentient beings and weighing whether or not to support animal consumption and cruel farming practices.

Living less selfishly is the ethical imperative. Regardless of what one may think about animal welfare, one can find reasons to feel good about eating less meat if only because it is virtually an ecological necessity. In order to live in a way which is sustainable for the entire world over the decades to come, it appears that the average individual might need to change their diet so that instead of deriving 20 percent of their protein from animal-based products, they would need to drop to 5 percent.

The average American diet consists in twice the protein than is actually needed, according to the Physician's Committee for Responsible Medicine. The USDA [US Department of Agriculture] estimates that a person weighing 150 lbs. requires 54 grams per day. While it is probably not realistic for most people to cut out all meat and dairy, a good place to start for most people would be to eat no more protein than is necessary to maintain good health, and to reduce the percentage of protein received from animal-based products. For many people integrating vegetarian or vegan protein supplements could help.

I am suggesting that eating benefits from taking a moral and philosophical approach which puts at the center the care of the spiral of evolution as a whole. For this reason, finding an integral path between the Vegetarian v. Carnivore options is a spiritual process. With conscious eating choices, we are impacting other sentient beings and weighing whether or not to support animal consumption and cruel farming practices.

Weighing the Labels

Worldcentric wisdom demands the practice of what we might call a "worldcentric diet" or "globally sustainable diet," which is similar to the identities of being a "near vegetarian" or "gradual vegetarian" or a "conscious carnivore." Why do we need to choose between these labels at all? It is time to stop asking people to identify with either vegetarianism or carnivorous behavior at all and start living at the edge of their capacity for healthful and ethical discernments.

Vegetarians may object: "But if someone eats meat at all, that disqualifies them by definition from being a vegetarian." The problem with this reply is that it assumes that an absolutistic definition of vegetarianism is fixed and immutable. Think about vegetarianism as a sort of "vegetable-philia," an ethos which says everything about how much one adores vegetables but which does not imply an exclusive commitment. An evolution in terms of our use of the term vegetarian would make it more useful.

And while no one ought to malign the movement to bring more consciousness to meat eaters, the term "conscious carnivore" isn't great. While it is intended to help shift food culture in positive directions, it still reinforces the notion that people are defined as carnivores simply by the inclusion of meat in their diet. People who eat meat also eat other sorts of foods and are accurately described as omnivorous. Perhaps the term "conscious omnivore" needs a boost as a replacement of both "vegetarian" and "carnivore," for it shifts the focus away from exclusivistic definitions and opens the door for fresh discussions.

CHAPTER 3

Are Vegetarian Diets More Humane than Diets That Include Meat?

Overview: The Evolution of Vegetarianism

Sari Kamin

Sari Kamin is an author and frequent contributor to the Heritage Radio Network.

Recently, on her weekly Heritage Radio Network program, "A Taste of the Past," Linda Pellacio interviewed Rynn Berry, an author and historical advisor to the North American Vegetarian Society.

Berry has been a vegetarian since learning, as a teenager, that animals experience anxiety before slaughter. His vegetarianism has since evolved into a vegan lifestyle, which means he excludes all animal products, including honey, not just from his diet but also from his clothing.

With Pellacio, Berry discussed the trajectory of vegetarianism, which has been a documented part of history since the sixth century B.C. According to Berry, the first vegetarian society was founded by the ancient Greek mathematician, Pythagoras (a key player in ninth grade geometry). Not only did Pythagoras demystify triangles, he also spread the gospel of the Buddha, a contemporary of Pythagoras who inspired him personally to practice non-violent vegetarianism. For Pythagoras, abstaining from meat was rooted in his spiritual values; nutrition would not become a factor in the diet until much later in history. In fact, a diet void of any animal products was actually called a "Pythagorean" diet until 1944, when Donald Watson, founder of the Vegan Society, coined the word vegan. Vegetarianism was first documented in 1848, most likely by an Oxford Scholar.

Famous Vegetarians from History

Berry has written several books on vegetarianism, including *Famous Vegetarians*. Notable meat-abstainers include Benjamin Franklin, whom Berry described as "the only founding father to have a fling with vegetarianism," as well as George Bernard Shaw, who was famously told by a team of doctors that he needed to eat meat or starve. Not only did he not starve, he lived until the age of 94.

Other vegetarians of the 19th century have had the legacy of their names enter the industrial food lexicon of today. John Harvey Kellogg, a Seventh-Day Adventist and the inventor of corn flakes, created the cereal as an alternative meatless breakfast option. Sylvester Graham, a Presbyterian minister who preached for temperance, whole grains, and vegetarian diets, created a cracker he believed was a nutritionally superior product. S'mores enthusiasts can rest assured that the modern version of the beloved campfire treat, the graham cracker, bears little resemblance to the original prototype.

Regardless of the choices you make in your diet, the more the dots are connected between health, compassion and ecology, the more nourishing your diet will become for your mind and your body.

The trajectory of vegetarianism is particularly interesting, especially in America, where history has recorded its renaissance on several occasions. The early vegetarians who I have named in this article were all inspired by their respective religions to cling to a meat-free diet. Their goals may have varied, but the common impetus was a spiritual sense of clarity that was thought to be achieved by eating a diet void of flesh. It wasn't until the 20th century that America embraced vegetarianism in a secular fashion. The baby-boomer generation, spurred by the violence of the 1960's and disparaged by threats of imminent ecological disasters, largely embraced a diet inspired by ecology and a desire to get closer to the Earth. By the time Frances Moore Lappé's iconic book, *Diet for a Small Planet* (1971), was published, vegetarianism had found its way into mainstream America's collective consciousness.

Modern Reasons for Vegetarianism

Today we are seeing a vegetarian redux. On one hand, nutrition is worshipped in society and a meat-free diet has become an acceptable entry point into a healthy lifestyle. Even extreme versions of vegetarianism, such as veganism and raw-food diets, have begun to shed their stigma. William Jefferson Clinton, who was not a founding father but is a beloved former president, has been outspoken about his drastic transition from a fast-food fueled diet to a strict vegan one. Rynn Berry would refer to Clinton as a "coronary vegetarian," someone who moves to a plant-based diet on the recommendation of their doctor after having a heart attack or a major procedure. Possibly inspired by their former president, or perhaps just riding the current trend wave, the American people have listened to a litany of testaments from celebrities who swear by their new meat-free diets. Rarely are ethics the impetus, and the nutrition-focused impulse has created a cross section of players on the corner of "I want my meat" and "I want to feel good about it too." This new business of wanting to stay healthy without sacrificing taste cravings has inspired movements such as "Meatless Mondays," which encourages a commitment to eating lower on the food chain without having to go cold turkey. Or cold tofurkey, as the case may be.

The ethical devotion to a cruelty-free diet, we can see, has been tempered and popularized by a re-shift of focus. Yes, we still care about animals, but now that we know that we can consume creatures that have lived healthy and happy lives, we no longer have to stress about their blood staying on our hands. It is important to note that only five percent of Americans identify themselves as vegetarians and for the majority of the population who are meat eaters, there are other ways to impact the environment and one's own health in a powerful and positive way. Pushing for breed diversity in our meat supply and purchasing only sustainably raised livestock are effective and important choices that meat-eaters should consider. Vegetarianism in itself is inherently complicated; the deep relationships between the livestock and dairy industries make for considerable debate when choosing to exclude meat from a diet but not cheese and milk. Regardless of the choices you make in your diet, the more the dots are connected between health, compassion and ecology, the more nourishing your diet will become for your mind and your body.

Pro-Animal, Pro-Life

Mary Eberstadt

Mary Eberstadt is a contributing writer to First Things *and a research fellow at the Hoover Institution. She is also the author of* Home-Alone America *and editor of* Why I Turned Right: Leading Baby Boom Conservatives Chronicle Their Political Journeys.

Why aren't vegetarians and pro-lifers more closely aligned? After all, the best writing about ethical vegetarianism— the moral case for refusing meat, as opposed to the more self-interested arguments from health or finance—is good enough to provoke serious reflection, even among nonvegetarians. Yet while this increasingly thoughtful literature flourishes, reflecting the movement of many Americans (especially younger ones) into the varieties of a meat-free diet, it has also proved a one-way street. Vegans and vegetarians do talk to one another, but usually without anyone in the rest of the world talking back—especially those committed to defending human life.

One reason for the current estrangement between vegetarians and moral traditionalists starts in the universities. Most academic thinking about vegetarianism and related dietary ethics today falls into two general pools of thought: utilitarianism and postmodern feminism. Both are hostile to the idea of admitting unborn *human* life to their circle of approved moral sympathy. As such, both have rendered themselves off limits to other serious people—those who draw their moral code from traditional Judeo-Christian thought—who might in different circumstances be open to persuasion.

Considering the Capacity to Suffer

The utilitarians, for their part, owe much to the work of Peter Singer. Singer's thesis, which is known almost as well among his adversaries as among his allies, is deceptively simple. Following Jeremy Bentham and other utilitarians who argued that the capacity to suffer is "the vital characteristic that gives a being a right to equal consideration," Singer takes the definition to its next step. "No matter what the nature of the being," as he puts it in his book *Animal Liberation*, "the principle of equality requires that its suffering be counted equally with the like suffering—insofar as rough comparisons can be made—of any other being." In short, when properly understood, animals have rights of the same sorts as humans—and in some cases, depending on the state of sentience, rights that trump those of certain humans. "Surely," as Singer puts it in one of many formulations often quoted by his adversaries, "there will be some nonhuman animals whose lives, by any standards, are more valuable than the lives of some humans."

For a spokesman who would persuade the world toward the practice of vegetarianism, [Peter] Singer has almost certainly lost many more potential practitioners of a "cruelty-free" diet than he has gained.

Though *admirable* is not the first word that leaps to mind when facing some of the practical consequences, Singer's theory does have the virtue of a ruthless consistency. We know this because, for decades now, the author has been spelling out the more malodorous of those consequences with some gusto. Perhaps most infamously, he has argued that, since a newborn infant lacks self-consciousness, autonomy, and rationality, "killing a newborn baby is never equivalent to killing a person, that is, a being who wants to go on living."

Along the way, Singer has alienated moral traditionalists, especially those concerned with abortion, more successfully than any other contemporary academic thinker—which is quite a feat. For good measure, he is also overtly hostile to Christianity, arguing that despite the relatively enlightened opinions of a few vegetarians—St. Basil, St. John Chrysostom, St. Isaac the Syrian—the Christian tradition is fatefully marred by its "exclusively speciesist preoccupation" with human beings.

For a spokesman who would persuade the world toward the practice of vegetarianism, Singer has almost certainly lost many more potential practitioners of a "cruelty-free" diet than he has gained. Subsequent utilitarians have generally followed in his antihumanist and pro-abortion steps. Tom Regan is perhaps the second-most prominent academic in the business of moralizing about animals, and in his influential 1981 book, *The Case for Animal Rights*, he proposes that, if humans have a natural right to life that is independent of their ability to be rational agents, then so too must animals.

Regan has been coy on the obvious question of whether his moral solicitude for nonrational animal life might logically extend to unborn human life. In a well-known essay called "Empty Cages," he does go so far as to refer, once, to what he calls "the terribly difficult question of the morality of abortion." But whether this terrible difficulty means that his philosophical principles might extend toward unborn human life as well as animal life is, apparently, off limits apart from that opaque observation.

Ecofeminism

In short, neither the grim consistency of Singer nor the reticence of Regan endears the utilitarian defenders of animals to anyone concerned with protecting unborn human life. And neither does the other set of academic ideas most commonly arrayed in vegetarianism's name: postmodern feminism.

Consider the work of Carol J. Adams, whose 1990 book *The Sexual Politics of Meat* was widely hailed even outside academia as an exciting new contribution to the theory of animal rights. Adams argues what has become the cornerstone of "ecofeminism": the notion that the so-called objectification of animals in a carnivorous society and the so-called objectification of women in a patriarchal society are somehow linked.

The claim may not be quite as novel as it sounds. Early women's-rights activists, such as Mary Wollstonecraft, were also advocates of kindness to animals, and Wollstonecraft saw her 1792 *Vindication of the Rights of Women* pilloried in an anonymous (and influential) publication called *A Vindication of the Rights of Brutes*. Many early feminists took up animal well-being as a related moral issue, and many people interested in animal well-being through the years have similarly made alliances with feminists.

The academic feminism concerned with animal suffering appears incapable of facing violence to the human fetus with an open mind.

Nonetheless, Adams' obfuscating postmodern language invites no comparison to the early feminists. Abounding in such terms as *absent referent* and *anarchovegan*, as well as in the usual hostility toward the other sex with which postmodern feminism is riddled, this kind of effort has little chance of persuading moral traditionalists. To most of them, Adams' work on behalf of animals would be just as repugnant as Peter Singer's—if it were anywhere near as readable.

The academic feminism concerned with animal suffering appears incapable of facing violence to the human fetus with an open mind. In a 1995 book called *Neither Man nor Beast: Feminism and the Defense of Animals*, Adams herself tackles the question of what an animal-rights theorist should make of abortion, only to conclude that appealing to the principle of nonviolence in both cases would be hypocritical: "As long as women and animals are ontologized as usable (rapable on the one hand and consumable on the other)," she explains, "both animal defense and abortion rights will be necessary."

Another representative foray into ecofeminism, a 1995 collection of essays called *Animals and Women: Theoretical Feminist Explorations*, exhibits a similar blindness to any moral connection between prerational human life and nonrational animal life. At times the backpedaling is so furious that one expects to see treadmarks on the page. "[Even] if we grant that the fetus is sentient (at least in some phases of its existence)," runs one typically contorted example, "or that the fetus is a rightholder in the sense that philosopher Tom Regan . . . contends, we are still confronted by the question as to who is the appropriate moral agent to resolve any potential conflict between the primary rightholder (the woman) and the subservient rightholder (the fetus). The only choices are to let the primary rightholder decide, or to relegate the responsibility to a legal system dominated by actors and ideologies that are inherently sexist."

Just how much of [PETA's] animal-liberation grand-standing is approved by actual vegetarians and vegans . . . is a question that never seems to get asked anywhere—and should be.

The sheer decibel level of unreason surrounding the issue of abortion in academic writing about animal rights tells us something interesting. It suggests that, contrary to what the utilitarians and feminists working this terrain wish, the dots between sympathy for animals and sympathy for unborn humans are in fact quite easy to connect—so easy, you might say, that a child could do it.

The Problem with PETA

There is another reason that vegetarians and their friends seem stuck in a ghetto far from moral traditionalists. This one concerns not theory but practice—the self-defeating and often obnoxious practice of political theater as pioneered by People for the Ethical Treatment of Animals (PETA), perhaps the leading headline hog in the pro-animal cause today.

PETA, as is not acknowledged nearly enough, has done much to discredit both vegetarianism and the humane treatment of animals. This is so not only among prolifers but also in the public more generally. The group is inescapably enamored of campaigns that make clear its own loyalty to the idea that man is just one of the animals—and emphatically a lower-order one at that. "Holocaust on Your Plate," an ad campaign equating leather and meat-eating with the extermination of the Jews, was one example. PETA's "Animal Liberation Project," comparing chimpanzees in cages to Africans, was another.

Just how much of this animal-liberation grandstanding is approved by *actual* vegetarians and vegans, as opposed to how much of it is mere political theater aimed at shocking what by now must be a shockproof bourgeoisie, is a question that never seems to get asked anywhere—and should be. It may well be true, as Wesley Smith has observed, that "the more radical elements of the movement increasingly resort to vandalism, arson, theft, violence, and intimidation in the name of protecting animals—and PETA has repeatedly refused to condemn such tactics."

Yet again, PETA's claim to represent actual vegans and vegetarians seems highly doubtful. Even Peter Singer has used his own status as éminence grise to warn against the fringe elements of the movement. "It would be a tragic mistake," he writes in his preface to the 1990 edition of *Animal Liberation*, "if even a small section of the Animal Liberation movement were to attempt to achieve its objectives by hurting people."

None of this is to say that the fringe movements purporting to benefit animals enjoy no support; clearly they do, in the same way that, say, the IRA [Irish Republican Army] at the peak of its violence enjoyed money and funds from at least some supporters who would never have dreamed of fashioning a Molotov cocktail of their own. But one hears little or nothing of such animal-liberation activism in the mainstream gathering places of vegetarianism, such as the International Vegetarian Union (IVU), let alone the more run-of-the-mill venues of interest to noncarnivores that are dominated instead by recipe sharing, health news, and personal-conversion stories.

One more reason for the impasse between vegetarians and pro-lifers needs to be noted. Conservatives, including religious traditionalists, have been generally disinclined to give vegetarian views a hearing. No less an authority than Richard John Neuhaus gently reprimanded readers a few years ago after receiving letters unhappy with the respectful review he had given to the book *Dominion*, Matthew Scully's evangelical case for vegetarianism. "Some readers," Fr. Neuhaus wrote, "think vegetarianism is so manifestly and self-evidently wrongheaded that, after rejecting it on first encounter, one would be a moral idiot to give it a second thought."

Vegetarianism is not easily dismissed either morally or intellectually, despite the fact that some traditionalists have relished doing just that for several decades now.

Much of that conservative dismissal, of course, is not about vegetarianism as such but about the baggage that has come to be associated with it. Certainly in the 1960s, vegetarianism was heavily identified as a hippie, fringe kind of movement with about as much moral force as tie-dying and ukulele strumming. Even though the movement has matured since its flower days, many vegetarians and vegans can be—like moral converts of any stripe—self-righteous and proselytizing to an annoying fault.

Other Objections to Vegetarianism

Yet leaving those historical accidents aside, what is there *intrinsically* about vegetarian practice for a moral traditionalist to object to? As a matter of history, over the centuries a number of serious Christians have spied a connection between vegetarianism and religious belief—a history that is somewhat at odds with the frequent conflation by conservatives of vegetarians with tree-hugging pagans.

The online sites devoted to Catholic vegetarianism claim numerous saints among their number—Francis of Assisi (though his vegetarianism appears in doubt), Clare, Martin de Porres, John Chrysostom, and Anthony of Padua among them. It is also a fact that Trappists, Cistercians, Benedictines, and Franciscans traditionally adopted vegetarian diets. Various other notables, East and West, have seen in vegetarianism a code congruent with spiritual beliefs. Both Mahatma Gandhi and Leo Tolstoy, among others, were not only vegetarians but ones who gave literary and religious accounts of their reasons for that practice.

In short, vegetarianism is not easily dismissed either morally or intellectually, despite the fact that some traditionalists have relished doing just that for several decades now. Like the boutique academic theorists speaking in vegetarianism's name, these traditionalists seem to have missed the moral forest for its more superficial trees.

My purpose in untangling these distinctions is not to put anyone in the moral dock, whether vegetarian or carnivore. It is rather to point out something easily overlooked—that there is more common moral ground between vegetarians and people concerned with the life issues than either side seems to realize.

Most people who adopt a vegetarian or cruelty-free diet do not do so on the basis of the antihumanist, anti-life ideas that prevail in academic thought. On the contrary, evidence abounds that most people change their dietary habits not because of carbon footprints or absent referents but through a very different process—acknowledging and acting on a moral intuition.

> *Since ethical vegetarianism as a practice appears commonly rooted in an a priori aversion to violence against living creatures, so does it often appear to begin in the young.*

This important point—overlooked, perhaps, precisely because it is so simple—is the moral key to a place where actual vegetarian lambs can easily be imagined resting alongside pro-life lions. Consider, for example, the explanation most commonly offered for vegetarianism. A 1989 book called *The New Vegetarian* found, after three hundred interviews, that 67 percent cited "concern for animal suffering" as the primary reason for their decision—by far the most common explanation. Similarly, in the 2006 *Vegans and Vegetarianism Today* (which features "Former Meat Eaters Tell Their Stories" as its first chapter), the editors emphasize that the "one path to vegetarianism" is defined as "the sudden, powerful emotional punch to the soul that people who have empathy, love, or just respect for animals feel upon discovering the details of the origins of meat."

"I told myself that I could no longer eat something that had at one time experienced the gift of life," one vegetarian writes online. "Vegetarianism fits with Christian ethical principles," adds another. "I'm against the maltreatment of animals," declares a third. These will not strike readers as terribly sophisticated explanations—which is exactly the point. They are not the arguments made by people who have been reasoned by esoterica into a new belief. They are explanations by people in possession of what they believe to be an intuitively appealing moral principle.

Children and Vegetarianism

Since ethical vegetarianism as a practice appears commonly rooted in an a priori aversion to violence against living creatures, so does it often appear to begin in the young. In an engaging collection of essays from 2001 called *Voices from the Garden: Stories of Becoming a Vegetarian*, editors Sharon and Daniel Towns observe of their fifty authors that "some were children when they realized that the meat on their plates came from the adorable duckies and lambs in their storybooks and on their bedroom curtains. Usually, but not always, a parent intervened and forced or persuaded the questioning child to be quiet and eat their dinner. Those children often grow up to think about the issue later in life, and, this time, to make their [vegetarian] pledge stick."

This same fact—that childhood insight writ large is a common denominator for many noncarnivores—is also observed by Matthew Scully. In *Dominion* he describes his own formative experience at age twelve of killing a baby bird to put it out of its misery, only to find himself "horrified at the bluntness of what I had done, obliterating this beautiful tiny creature so finely made who tried so hard to live." Such childhood epiphanies, as he perceives, are common among vegetarians and others concerned with animal protection—indeed, they are perhaps the most common denominator of all, as Scully himself notes: "I once asked a friend who is prominently involved in the animal-rights movement what it was that got him started. He said that, from the time he was a child, he could not bear the thought of animal suffering, of the helplessness of any creature subjected to cruelty.... That original motivation, that basic conviction common to so many people in the rights cause, perhaps runs deeper than any theory they might profess."

In 2002, Richard John Neuhaus, though no vegetarian, affirmed this same point with his own personal story of youthful epiphany about animals. "This twelve-year-old," he relates, "had deep thoughts about our rights to pork chops and bacon" when faced with the actual slaughter of the farm's prize hog. Neuhaus was not entirely persuaded by Scully's and related arguments; he went on to suggest a limited defense of meat eating and a call to regulatory intervention into the crueler factory farming practices. Even so, he cautioned readers against dismissing in principle the budding moral sentiments of our twelve-year-old selves. "Such reactions," he cautioned Scully's critics, "are not to be brushed aside as juvenile squeamishness but should be thought through with care."

In a recent pitch for veganism, *The Face on Your Plate*, Jeffrey Masson relates in the opening how, when teaching Sanskrit at the University of Toronto in the 1970s, "I came across a phrase that stopped me dead: *ashrayaparavrtti*—a sudden moment of life-changing insight." The reason he was so struck by the phrase was its resonance with his own experience and that of others about their decision to embrace vegetarianism. "Many people," he observes, "become vegan in just that way: a sudden moment, a blinding insight, a turning of one's back on conventional wisdom."

The line connecting the dots between "we should respect animal life" and "we should respect human life" is far straighter than the line connecting vegetarianism to anti-life feminism or antihumanist utilitarianism.

All of which brings us to the deepest point that so many vegetarians and moral traditionalists seem to have overlooked through the years, and why it seems fair to speak of a missed moral opportunity between the two.

A sudden insight, igniting empathy on a scale that did not exist before and perhaps even a life-transforming realization—this reaction should indeed be thought through with care. It is not only the most commonly cited feature of the decision to become a vegetarian. It is also the most commonly cited denominator of what brings people to their convictions about the desperate need to protect unborn, innocent human life.

Joseph Bottum, for one, has memorably described just such an epiphany in an essay for a book I edited called *Why I Turned Right*. In his case, it came knocking one day when, as a student in the Georgetown library, he sat watching idly through the window as a mother wrestled fruitlessly with her dog, leash, and baby stroller. All the while, as he watched, the baby laughed with delight, "clapping her small hands at the slapstick world into which God and her parents had unexpectedly delivered her." Enter what Masson identifies as the *ashrayaparavrtti*: "It was at that moment," Bottum writes, that there arrived "the sudden, absolute conviction that babies are good. . . . Always for me it comes back to this touchstone: Anything that participates in the murder of a child . . . is wrong. All the rest is just a working out of the details."

Many other pro-life writers and activists—prominent or not, religious believers or not—have related similar formative experiences. Fred Barnes has written that his own moment came in a doctor's office with his pregnant wife, as they contemplated for the first time the real meaning of amniocentesis. My own Damascan moment (described in the same volume where Bottum's essay appears) remains vivid for me in every detail: Cornell University, 1980, watching a circus-atmosphere debate between a small-town Baptist preacher and a ferociously pro-abortion tenured Marcusian feminist. Wesley J. Smith, one of America's most eloquent opponents of the culture of death, had a different kind of epiphany; it was the suicide of an ailing friend that prompted him to rethink and redirect his life.

For a great many other people, too, as one hears often at pro-life rallies, moral intuition about abortion was sparked by quotidian events—that first picture of an aborted fetus, the birth of their own first child, and the first moment of watching a fetus move on a sonogram. As with the vegetarians, once such an insight is digested and acted on, few people turn back to where they were before—a fact that speaks as no other could to the transformative power of the insight in question.

And therein lies the real key to a possible vegetarianism that casts off its utilitarian and feminist baggage to embrace a more logically consistent approach to creation. Despite those who act and write in their name, actual vegetarians and vegans are far more likely to be motivated by positive feelings for animals than by negative feelings for human beings. As a matter of theory, the line connecting the dots between "we should respect animal life" and "we should respect human life" is far straighter than the line connecting vegetarianism to antilife feminism or antihumanist utilitarianism. Any moral intuition powerful enough to cause second thoughts about a widely accepted practice—and to re-shape personal behavior accordingly—is an intuition that religious believers ordinarily take seriously indeed.

How could they not? Moral traditionalists recognize and value such intuitions readily enough when a child points to a picture of a fetus and says "baby" (as all children do). Theirs is the correct instinct, and so is our valuing of it. Why shouldn't the instinctive repulsion that some of them feel to eating the animals they've just petted on the farm not spring from the same pure stream of conscience—or at least be similar food for moral thought in the rest of us?

None of this is to introduce a moral equivalency between killing animals and killing humans—let alone to imply that moral sentiment, especially when fleeting, is a sufficient foundation for the good. As Hadley Arkes among others has wisely observed, moral sentiment was unreliable in the case of slavery—to which we might add many other examples of how custom can successfully blunt what may once have been the stirrings of real conscience, thus leading us on various fronts into grossest error.

Even so, if we turn our eyes away from the detour into antihumanism taken by prominent activists on behalf of vegetarianism—if we keep our eyes fixed instead on what it is that has actually drawn a significant number of individuals to the *practice* of vegetarianism—then we can see something unexpected and important: Vegetarians and pro-lifers are strangers to one another for reasons of accident rather than essence, and they also, furthermore, have a natural bond in moral intuitionism that should make them allies.

The work of developing that bond could be done, and the benefit might be immense for both sides—like finding a few million friends that you never knew you had.

Vegetables Can Be
Grown Without the Use
of Animal Products

John Walker

John Walker is a gardening and environmental writer, book author, and blogger who resides in the United Kingdom.

If you're expecting a delivery of steaming manure this spring, if you swear by pelleted poultry manure, or regularly use bonemeal or hoof and horn, you are, whether through ignorance or indifference, party to some pretty grisly goings-on: 'There are two types of captive bolt pistol: penetrative and non-penetrative. Penetrative stunners drive a bolt into the skull and cause unconsciousness both through physical brain damage and the concussive blow to the skull. The bolt on a non-penetrative stunner is "mushroom-headed" and impacts on the brain without entering the skull. Unconsciousness is caused by the concussive blow. Traditionally, animals are stunned before their throats are cut but the stun does not actually kill the animal. Animals die from loss of blood after their throats are cut.'

Most of us have never been inside a slaughterhouse, but it does not take much imagination. Such activities are a fact of everyday life (and death) in our food industry. And another fact of life is our long-established use, as gardeners, of the by-products of that industry.

Ethical Dilemma

Mostly, we gardeners tend to care deeply for the natural systems around us, of which we are part. If we tread a more earth-friendly, organic path, we aim to work with nature, not against it, to create healthy, biologically diverse and balanced ecosystems within our gardens and allotments. In tandem with that we recycle feverishly and shun synthetic pesticides. We get a buzz not just from the beneficial insect life we draw to our plots, but from the feeling that what we do has an ethical dimension; gardening in an earth-friendly way is an inherently 'good thing'. But how many of us, whatever our approach, have stopped to consider, wrapped in the steam rising from a barrowful of manure, the less ethical side to what we do?

Happily, a new way of growing is emerging that frees us from garden-scale ethical dilemmas. It is a way of growing that breaks our deep-seated reliance on animal by-products, be it their waste materials, ground-up parts of their carcasses, or the blood that flows through their veins. It's still earth-friendly, organic gardening at heart, but with added ethics. It has the potential to turn our gardens an even deeper shade of green, to make them more compassionate and to change the way we think about the world and our place in it. With a growing consensus that we should start to eat less meat to ease the growing environmental burden of the global livestock industry, it offers tomorrow's gardeners—for which steaming muck heaps might be a rare sight—a practical solution.

Virtually all of the fertility required to grow crops is generated within the holding, largely from composted plant wastes and the effective use of green manure crops.

As a long-time, occasionally faltering vegetarian with vegan leanings, I have resorted to using very few animal inputs in my new garden. This, I admit, grew more out of local necessity than a desire to avoid the lurking spectre of the slaughterhouse trade—sheep just don't do steaming manure heaps. Instead, I am composting like mad (both kitchen/household resources and the abundant bracken around my garden) and have occasionally topped up with soil improver from a local 'green waste' composting project.

When it comes to adding major plant nutrients, of which my virgin soil has virtually none, I now find myself passing over the 'classic' organic animal-derived fertilisers in favour of their more 'ethical' equivalents. Some of these come in seed packets, rather than fertiliser sacks.

Vegan-Organic Pioneers

This emerging way of growing plants is known as 'vegan-organic' or 'stock-free organic', signifying that soil fertility is maintained without the need for livestock or their by-products. It is being pioneered in the UK [United Kingdom] by a small but growing number of market gardeners who use zero animal inputs to run their businesses. They use no manure of any kind, nor any 'organic' fertilisers derived from the bodies of animals. Even the seed and potting composts they use are free of animal by-products. Demand is growing for food which is certified organic and which is, in addition, grown without the use of animal inputs—food, if you like, with impeccable moral credentials.

These growers use what is called a 'closed' system, meaning that virtually all of the fertility required to grow crops is generated within the holding, largely from composted plant wastes and the effective use of green manure crops, deployed via carefully planned crop rotations of up to nine years. Little, if anything, is brought into the loop.

Building Soil Fertility

Green manures—plants we grow to feed and build soil—are familiar to many gardeners, but we have as yet only scratched the surface of their potential to build fertility by increasing the soil's organic matter content, while enhancing our garden ecosystems. Put simply, green manures create fertility for free by trapping sunlight and building biomass in soil by increasing its bank of humus—a kind of dark, supercharged organic matter. The term 'green manure' often foxes gardeners hearing it for the first time. It's time for a makeover: 'fertility-building crops' gets to the nub.

Another key element of the vegan-organic approach is to minimise soil cultivation, to encourage a settled and balanced soil ecosystem. Soil which receives only light surface cultivation is ideal for the one kind of livestock that vegan-organic growers and gardeners do actively encourage: earthworms.

It's not hard to see that by declaring our plots 'animal by-product-free zones', we're gardening in a deeper green way and, ultimately, to an even higher set of values.

When green manures are a key part of your soil-building programme, more lateral, imaginative thinking kicks in, leading to some eye-catching partnerships. One of the cleverest I've tried is sweetcorn under-sown with the green manure buckwheat, which is sown at the same time as the sweetcorn is planted. The latter eventually towers above the buckwheat and while its tassels are busy shedding clouds of pollen overhead, the buckwheat is busy smothering weeds, its roots are increasing soil fertility, and its blooms are pulling in swarms of beneficial insects such as hoverflies, whose larvae eat aphids. The best bit about this combo is it works just as well in a garden or allotment.

Deeper Green

It would be naive to think that if all gardeners gave up using animal by-products fewer animals would have a penetrative stunner entering their skulls. But it still feels good to know I am on course to create a garden that has not relied heavily on distant, unseen slaughter. You don't need to become a vegan overnight (or indeed at all) to garden this way; it's an evolving way of growing that anyone, whatever their dietary preferences, can try out.

Being vegetarian, I realise I am guilty of inherent hypocrisy in that I still eat a few animal products, knowing full well that those animals, even if organically reared, are unlikely to end their days in sun-soaked retirement. Whatever the moral conundrums and ethical debates around what we choose to eat, it's not hard to see that by declaring our plots 'animal by-product-free zones', we're gardening in a deeper green way and, ultimately, to an even higher set of values.

Animals Suffer Needlessly for Food Production

Ted Genoways

Ted Genoways is a poet, a contributing writer at Mother Jones, *and an editor-at-large at* OnEarth.

Shawn Lyons was dead to rights—and he knew it. More than a month had passed since People for the Ethical Treatment of Animals (PETA) had released a video of savage mistreatment at the MowMar Farms hog confinement facility where he worked as an entry-level herdsman in the breeding room. The three enormous sow barns in rural Greene County, Iowa, were less than five years old and, until recently, had raised few concerns. They seemed well ventilated and well supplied with water from giant holding tanks. Their tightly tacked steel siding always gleamed white in the sun. But the PETA hidden-camera footage shot by two undercover activists over a period of months in the summer of 2008, following up on a tip from a former employee, showed a harsh reality concealed inside.

MowMar Farms

The recordings caught one senior worker beating a sow repeatedly on the back with a metal gate rod, a supervisor turning an electric prod on a sow too crippled to stand, another worker shoving a herding cane into a sow's vagina. In one close-up, a distressed sow who'd been attacking her piglets was shown with her face royal blue from the Prima Tech marking dye sprayed into her nostrils "to get the animal high." In perhaps the most disturbing sequence, a worker demonstrated the method for euthanizing underweight piglets: taking them by the hind legs and smashing their skulls against the concrete floor—a technique known as "thumping." Their bloodied bodies were then tossed into a giant bin, where video showed them twitching and paddling until they died, sometimes long after. Though his actions were not nearly as vicious as those of some coworkers who'd been fired immediately, Lyons knew, as the video quickly became national news, that the consequences for him could be severe.

Lyons was the first person ever convicted of criminal livestock neglect on a Midwestern farm—and only the seventh person convicted of animal abuse in the history of the American meat industry.

As we sat recently in the tiny, tumbledown house he grew up in and now shares with his wife and two kids, Lyons acknowledged—as he did to the sheriff's deputy back then—that he had prodded sows with clothespins, hit them with broad, wooden herding boards, and pulled them by their ears, but only in an effort, he said, to get pregnant sows that had spent the last 114 days immobilized in gestation crates up and moving to the farrowing crates where they would give birth. Lyons said he never intended to hurt the hogs, that he was just "scared to death" of the angry sows "who had spent their lives in a little pen"—and this was how he had been trained to deal with them. Lyons had watery blue eyes that seemed always on the verge of tears and spoke in a skittish mutter that would sometimes disappear all the way into silence as he rubbed his thin beard. "You do feel sorry for them, because they don't have much room to move around," he said, but if they get spooked coming out of their crates, "you're in for a fight."

Lyons had been trained in these methods of hog-handling (many of them, including thumping, legal and widely practiced), but a spokeswoman for Hormel—one of the largest food processors in the country and the dominant buyer of MowMar's hogs—had already called the video "appalling" and "completely unacceptable," and MowMar's owners had responded by vowing that any additional workers found guilty of abuse as authorities pored over the tape would be terminated. Still, it came as a surprise when his boss informed him that he had been formally charged and immediately fired. "We don't want to do it," the supervisor told him, "but we got to—because Hormel will quit taking the sows." He told Lyons to turn himself in at the courthouse.

While Lyons filled out paperwork and had his mug shot taken, his wife's cellphone buzzed again and again: Her husband's name was already on the evening news. Lyons hired a lawyer—but he was on video and he'd confessed to the deputy sheriff.

"They got you, dude," Lyons said his attorney told him. He accepted a plea agreement—six months' probation and a $625 fine plus court fees—and signed an admission of guilt. It may seem like a slap on the wrist, but Lyons was the first person ever convicted of criminal livestock neglect on a Midwestern farm—and only the seventh person convicted of animal abuse in the history of the American meat industry. He wasn't alone for long: Five of Lyons' coworkers, soon signed similar agreements.

A Hollow Victory

It was a major PR [public relations] win for PETA—which often appeals to local authorities to make arrests but rarely gets the kind of cooperation they got from the Greene County Sheriff's Office—but it was also a hollow victory. "Who in their right mind would want to work in a dusty, ammonia-ridden pig shed for nine bucks an hour but somebody who, literally, had no other options?" asked Dan Paden, the senior researcher at PETA who helped run the investigation. "And at the end of a long, frustrating day, when you are trying to move a pig who hasn't been out of its crate in [months], that's when these beatings occur—and people do stupid, cruel, illegal things." PETA was urging prosecutors to go beyond plea agreements for farmworkers; they wanted charges against farm owners and their corporate backers, to hold them responsible for crimes committed by undertrained, overburdened employees.

This prospect scared industrial-scale meat producers into organizing a coordinated pushback. Recognizing that, in the era of smartphones and social media, any worker could easily shoot and distribute damning video, meat producers began pressing for legislation that would outlaw this kind of whistleblowing. Publicly, MowMar pledged to institute a zero-tolerance policy against abuse and even to look into installing video monitoring in its barns. And yet last summer, at the World Pork Expo in Des Moines, MowMar's co-owner Lynn Becker recommended that each farm hire a spokesperson to "get your side of the story out" and called the release of PETA's video "the 9/11 event of animal care in our industry."

Ag gag laws . . . don't just interfere with workers blowing the whistle on animal abuse. "You are also stopping environmental whistleblowing; you are also stopping workers' rights whistleblowing."

As overheated as likening that incident to a terrorist attack may seem, such thinking has become woven into the massive lobbying effort that agribusiness has launched to enact a series of measures known (in a term coined by the *New York Times'* Mark Bittman) as ag gag. Though different in scope and details, the laws (enacted in 8 states and introduced in 15 more) are viewed by many as undercutting—and even criminalizing—the exercise of First Amendment rights by investigative reporters and activists, whom the industry accuses of "animal and ecological terrorism."

Using a legal cudgel to go after critics wasn't entirely a new tactic for agribusiness. PETA first began undercover investigations around 1981—getting video of rhesus monkeys being vivisected in a Maryland medical research lab by posing as employees—and a few legislatures responded by enacting laws to protect animal research from exposés. (Only Kansas had the foresight to expand its law to cover "livestock and domestic animals.") Then, in 1992, when two ABC *PrimeTime Live* reporters shot undercover video of Food Lion workers in the Carolinas repackaging spoiled meat, Food Lion sued—not for libel, since the tapes spoke for themselves, but for fraud and trespass, because the reporters had submitted false information on their job applications. (A jury awarded $5.5 million, but an appeals court reduced it to just $2.) In 1996, at the height of the mad cow scare, the Texas Beef Group launched a two-year lawsuit against Oprah Winfrey over an episode that questioned the safety of hamburger. Recently, not only has the rhetoric heated up, but so has the coordinated legislative effort. Deeply invested in industrywide methods that a growing number of consumers find distasteful or even cruel, agribusiness has united in making sure that prying eyes literally don't see how the sausage is made.

Farms and Self-Regulation

"If you think this is an animal welfare issue, you have missed the mark," said Amanda Hitt, director of the Government Accountability Project's Food Integrity Campaign, who served as a representative for the whistleblowers who tipped off ABC in the Food Lion case. "This is a bigger, broader issue." She likened activist videos to airplane black-box recorders—evidence for investigators to deconstruct and find wrongdoing. Ag gag laws, she said, don't just interfere with workers blowing the whistle on animal abuse. "You are also stopping environmental whistleblowing; you are also stopping workers' rights whistleblowing." In short, "you have given power to the industry to completely self-regulate." That should "scare the pants off" consumers concerned about where their food comes from. "It's the consumer's right to know, but also the employee's right to tell. You gotta have both.". . .

The bill sailed through the Senate by unanimous consent, and in the House encountered resistance only from Rep. Dennis Kucinich (D-Ohio). Kucinich warned it would "have a chilling effect on the exercise of the constitutional rights of protest," before a voice vote on the bill allowed it to be ushered through.

Workers at the Willmar Poultry Company—the country's largest turkey hatchery, producing 45 million birds a year—were filmed by HSUS undercover activists throwing sick, injured, and surplus birds into grinding machines while still alive.

Application of the law soon nipped at the heels of the First Amendment. Most notably, a jury found a New Jersey chapter of a UK [United Kingdom]-based anti-animal-testing group guilty of conspiracy for publishing the home addresses of researchers at Huntingdon Life Sciences—handing down convictions for seven, including the chapter's webmaster. The case was chronicled in a low-budget documentary called *Your Mommy Kills Animals*, which discussed the case for prosecuting animal rights activist groups, including PETA and the Humane Society of the United States (HSUS), as homegrown terrorist organizations. The movie was underwritten by über-lobbyist Richard Berman, who runs the Center for Consumer Freedom and was immortalized by *60 Minutes* as "Dr. Evil." Because nonprofits don't have to reveal their donor lists, it's impossible to know exactly how much money Berman takes in from particular corporations. However, a canceled check for $50,000, introduced as part of a lawsuit resulting from the documentary, revealed that Hormel was a backer—and Berman described in testimony as a "supporter." (Berman sued the filmmakers because, contrary to his wishes, they made a movie that was too evenhanded.)

Criminalizing Undercover Video

By early 2011, there was another run at introducing state-level laws that would expand the definition of "enterprise interference" to include shooting undercover video. It came after Joe C. Swedberg, vice president for legislative affairs at Hormel, invited Minnesota House Majority Whip Rod Hamilton and state Sen. Doug Magnus, chairs of their respective agricultural committees, to jointly deliver the policy lecture at the Minnesota Agri-Growth Council. The council sees its mission as shaping the legislative agenda; Swedberg was then board chairman. Magnus was former chairman of the United Soybean Board; Hamilton had been president of the Minnesota Pork Producers Association and worked in communications for Christensen Family Farms, the third-largest pork producer in the United States. Swedberg and Hamilton had previously served together on Gov. Tim Pawlenty's Livestock Advisory Task Force and a legislative commission on immigration.

The talk, according to the Agri-Growth Council's newsletter, drew one of the largest and most varied arrays of attendees in the group's history. Ten weeks later, Hamilton and Magnus introduced identical bills that would make it a crime to "produce a record which reproduces an image or sound" inside an animal facility—or even "possess or distribute" such a recording. Daryn McBeth, the president of the Agri-Growth Council, told the Minneapolis *Star Tribune* that the law would be "an important deterrent tool in our toolbox" against videos shot by "fraudulently hired employees." The *Star Tribune* pointed to a case that rocked Minnesota a few months earlier, when workers at the Willmar Poultry Company—the country's largest turkey hatchery, producing 45 million birds a year—

were filmed by HSUS undercover activists throwing sick, injured, and surplus birds into grinding machines while still alive.

It was a spotlight on another horrifying but legal practice. . . .

Since 1980, Nebraska has lost 91 percent of its independent hog producers, 80 percent of its dairy producers and 40 percent of its beef producers. . . . It was not HSUS that drove them out of business. What drove them out of business was a market increasingly controlled by multinational food corporations.

Meanwhile, in what some animal rights activists have called an "evolutionary change" in strategy, Missouri and Nebraska lawmakers introduced bills that include provisions for what is termed "quick reporting"—a concept ostensibly intended to protect animals, but that de facto makes it impossible for journalists or activists to build a convincing case of sustained abuse. Under some of these new provisos, activists or whistleblowers would be required to submit written reports of any signs of abuse they witnessed and all supporting evidence to authorities within a matter of hours—or face criminal charges themselves. Whistleblowers would not even be allowed to keep any copies of materials they submitted to authorities. Critics say the measures are a cynical warping of so-called good Samaritan measures that require reporting child abuse or sexual assault. Only in this case, by analogy, a teacher who later came to suspect child abuse could be prosecuted for not reporting the first bump or bruise.

"It's absurd," said Amanda Hitt at the Government Accountability Project. She said she couldn't believe that an industry that has been so regularly recorded breaking the law "would then have the audacity to come to any state legislative body and say, 'Hey, we're sick of getting caught doing crimes. Could you do us a favor and criminalize catching us?'"

But that's exactly what has happened in Nebraska—under the guise of a new advocacy group called We Support Agriculture. In 2010, the Nebraska Cattlemen, Nebraska Farm Bureau, Nebraska Poultry Industries, Nebraska Pork Producers Association, and Nebraska State Dairy Association formed the organization to "defend the responsible animal welfare practices of Nebraska's farmers and ranchers from attacks by outside animal rights extremist groups." The effort was fraught with scandal from the start. First, the group received a $100,000 grant of taxpayer funds from Nebraska Attorney General Jon Bruning (who was running for US Senate at the time)—even though it didn't yet have employees, offices, or initiatives of any kind. It later came to light that Bruning approved the grant via email just 32 minutes after the request was submitted. Since then, the *Omaha World-Herald* has uncovered 1,800 phone calls, many of them late at night, between the group's first executive director, its only employee, and Nebraska's married lieutenant governor, Rick Sheehy. (Sheehy resigned over the scandal involving this and other relationships in February.)

Despite the controversy, We Support Agriculture has pressed ahead with distributing material disparaging animal rights activists supplied by none other than Richard Berman and the Center for Consumer Freedom. Ron Meyer, a cattle rancher who attended an early We Support Agriculture meeting, said local meat producers were told that the goal of the Humane Society of the United States was "to destroy animal agriculture and force everyone to become either vegetarian or vegan." But Meyer said that the HSUS spokesman he met in 2011 was a hog producer from Missouri and that 95 percent of HSUS supporters eat meat. "Since 1980, Nebraska has lost 91 percent of its independent hog producers, 80 percent of its dairy producers and 40 percent of its beef producers," Meyer wrote in an editorial for the *Lincoln Journal Star*. "It was not HSUS that drove them out of business. What drove them out of business was a market increasingly controlled by multinational food corporations that include the large meatpackers, which destroyed competitive and fair prices and operate with no transparency." Still, We Support Agriculture has enjoyed the steadfast support of Gov. Dave Heineman (who said of the HSUS: "We're going to kick your ass and send you out of the state") and a 27-year-old, Georgetown-educated state senator named Tyson Larson. . . .

The push for ag gag is not about concealing illegal abuse; it's about keeping the public from questioning whether legal, industry-standard practices should be allowed.

New Producers Bring Surprising Profits

Lynn Becker, head of LB Pork, describes his hog operation outside Fairmont, Minnesota, as a "good old-fashioned American family farm"—and it might appear that way at first. Everything about the place bespeaks its age, from the weathered, brick-red Dutch Gambrel barn to the simple farmhouse that Becker's grandfather built in the 1930s. But, in truth, Becker is the head of a giant operation. By 2008, when he bought into the MowMar facility, he was bringing more than 120,000 pigs to market annually; today, it's 156,000. The company is sprawling and complex, employing dozens of full-time and part-time workers spread out over 20 sites in Minnesota and Iowa.

Becker notes that the majority of the abuses captured on the PETA video occurred before his ownership, and he points to significant improvements in the last five years. Employees at the facility, renamed Fair Creek, now watch weekly training videos on a large flat-screen TV in the break room, where they are reminded of the fundamentals of "day one" piglet care. Piglets are now kept warm with heat lamps, and sows are moved much less frequently. "We try to leave pigs home with

Mom," Becker's health manager told the *National Hog Farmer*. "Never move more pigs than you have to." The new system has dramatically reduced piglet mortality rates—and, according to one worker, runts are now euthanized via the carbon monoxide system preferred by PETA, rather than the blunt-force thumping of old. "I didn't completely buy into it when we first started focusing on day one pig care," said the new farm manager, "but it really works."

In an era where we are all beginning to see the effects of letting industries regulate themselves—from the Deepwater Horizon spill to Wall Street's meltdown to spinach recalls—people are asking legitimate questions about the safety of their food supply.

These changes have not only improved conditions for the hogs at the facility in Iowa, but they have also helped increase the profit margin for its owners. Thus, in the end, improved care has been touted as a win for everyone. But would it have occurred without the harsh light of public scrutiny? And why does the industry want to criminalize outside oversight if it leads to higher profits, as well as improved animal care? These are not merely academic questions. In February [2013], the first person was charged under Utah's ag gag law. She was filming from a public road as a slaughterhouse attempted to move a sick cow with a tractor. The cops arrived within minutes; the co-owner of the meatpacker is also the mayor. The charges were swiftly dropped after journalist Will Potter publicized the case—but, it should be noted, had the tractor been moving the cow toward the abattoir for processing, then the woman would have been documenting a crime, an act nearly identical to the one that touched off the largest ground-beef recall in US history in 2008.

Why would the industry possibly want to protect a few bad actors at the risk of major expense and public outcry? According to the Government Accountability Project's Hitt, the push for ag gag is not about concealing illegal abuse; it's about keeping the public from questioning whether legal, industry-standard practices should be allowed.

"Some of these standard operating procedures are things that the general public doesn't like," Hitt said, "and, if by viewing them, your potential customer is turned off, then it is incumbent upon the industry to make changes." Take the use of gestation crates. When public opinion turned against keeping sows in nearly four-month-long confinement during pregnancy, the big producers were quick to change—with Smithfield and Hormel among the first to demand that their suppliers retrofit their operations. It's to avoid these kinds of costly PR nightmares, Hitt said, that industry has pushed to keep consumers from seeing how their food is raised and made.

But the ag gag campaign has come at another kind of cost for the industry. Bills to criminalize undercover investigations have created the impression that something brutal—and potentially illegal—is still going on inside facilities like Fair Creek. I asked Becker if the industry might not be better served by increased transparency, rather than tightened security. Why not open up the operation to journalists to prove that it no longer resembles the days when it was MowMar Farms? He gave a list of reasons—sow health, proprietary practices—it wouldn't be possible. Months of follow-up requests have gone unanswered.

It's not hard to see why such evasiveness makes the public uneasy. In an era where we are all beginning to see the effects of letting industries regulate themselves—from the Deepwater Horizon spill to Wall Street's meltdown to spinach recalls—people are asking legitimate questions about the safety of their food supply. With federal regulatory agencies now hobbled by spending cuts, the secrecy and impunity afforded by ag gag could send meat production back to the days of *The Jungle*.

Shawn Lyons, who spent two years unemployed after being fired from MowMar Farms, finally got a job with a security company. He installs video cameras in hospitals, nursing homes, and schools for 24-hour monitoring. Before I packed up my things and left his tiny house, Lyons asked me whatever became of Becker's promise to investigate security cameras for his hog barns. "That's what I do now," he said.

His wife, Sherri, chimed in. "They could have some kind of a committee set up that can come in and check anytime that they want, someone that's not associated with the company. I think that would be the better way to do it. So that people are well aware of the fact that there's cameras here, and there's this group of people that can come in anytime and look. So, you know, be on your best behavior."

Vegetarians May Be Responsible for More Animal Deaths than Omnivores

Julia Galef

Julia Galef is a New York-based writer and public speaker specializing in science, rationality, and design.

The most common justification I hear for vegetarianism is "It's wrong to kill an animal for food." Of course there are other motivations, such as health, religion, environmentalism, preventing suffering, and trying to score with liberal chicks— but the moral wrongness of killing an animal for food is probably the most common, at least in my experience.

Consequently, I've found it surprising that people so rarely acknowledge that vegetarians *do* kill millions of animals for food. If you buy eggs or milk or cheese, it's true in theory that the dairy cows and laying hens don't have to be killed in order to supply you with those products, but in practice, they are. A modern factory farm isn't just going to let their animals die of old age; they kill them at whatever point the farm considers to be the most profit-maximizing. For dairy cows, that's usually at age 3–5, out of a natural 20–25 year lifespan. For egg-laying hens, it's usually after one or two laying cycles. And since the males of the laying species are useless to the egg farmer, they're killed right after they hatch.

But surely eating a vegetarian diet must kill far fewer animals than an omnivore diet, right? Well . . . sort of. I'm sure that a *typical* vegetarian kills fewer animals than a *typical* omnivore. But it's certainly possible to be a vegetarian and kill more animals than an omnivore, and in fact, I'm confident that many vegetarians fall into that category.

Lives per Calorie

The culprit is eggs. While you only need to kill one single steer to get about 450 pounds (405,000 calories) worth of meat, you'd need to kill about 20 chickens to get enough eggs to match that number of calories. So if you're a vegetarian who eats a lot of omelets, you're likely responsible for more animal deaths than someone who chows down on burgers and steaks but doesn't like eggs.

Laying hens arguably lead some of the most miserable lives out of all livestock, spending all their time crammed into cages with less space than half a piece of paper.

I've scrounged up data on the typical amount of meat, eggs, and dairy that we get out of a modern farm animal, and combined it with data on the calorie counts of those foods. That allowed me to calculate the number of calories of food that we get out of each type of animal, or more to the point, the "lives-per-calorie" statistic for each food. [Results from omitted table ordered from "kills fewest animals per calorie" to "kills the most animals per calorie": milk/dairy cow, cheese/dairy cow, beef/steer, pork/hog, eggs/laying hen, chicken/broiler chicken.]

The lives-per-calories cost of eggs [0.048485 lives per 1000 calories] is so many times higher than that of beef [0.002469 lives per 1000 calories] that even a small amount of eggs outweighs the life cost of a larger amount of beef. So let's say you're a vegetarian and you go out to lunch with your omnivorous friend, where he orders a burger and you order an egg-salad sandwich. The two eggs in your sandwich are only 150 calories, compared to the 300 calories in his beef patty, but the eggs cost almost 9 times as much life as the beef.

Of course, as I said earlier, these calculations are only concerned with the question of taking animals' lives. They don't take into account the amount of suffering the animal experiences. That would change the calculations somewhat, but I suspect the overall verdict would remain similar if you were looking at suffering-per-calorie—or, if anything, things would look even grimmer for egg-lovers. Laying hens arguably lead some of the most miserable lives out of all livestock, spending all their time crammed into cages with less space than half a piece of paper, having their beaks cut off, and being starved to induce molting. (Although the male chicks would count less if you're looking at suffering-per-calorie, since their lives are so short.)

These calculations also don't take into account the impact on the environment. Raising beef is pretty clearly the worst industry in terms of things like producing greenhouse gases, breeding antibiotic-resistant bacteria, and requiring huge amounts of farmland just to feed the cattle. So there's still a good case for choosing eggs over beef in the sense of minimizing your environmental impact, but that doesn't change the fact that you'd be making a tradeoff: killing more animals to hurt the environment less.

Vegetarian Diets Cause More Animal Cruelty than Eating Meat

Mike Archer

Mike Archer is a professor at the University of New South Wales (UNSW) and part of UNSW's Evolution of Earth and Life Systems Research Group.

The ethics of eating red meat have been grilled recently by critics who question its consequences for environmental health and animal welfare. But if you want to minimise animal suffering and promote more sustainable agriculture, adopting a vegetarian diet might be the worst possible thing you could do.

Renowned ethicist Peter Singer says if there is a range of ways of feeding ourselves, we should choose the way that causes the least unnecessary harm to animals. Most animal rights advocates say this means we should eat plants rather than animals.

It takes somewhere between two to ten kilos of plants, depending on the type of plants involved, to produce one kilo of animal. Given the limited amount of productive land in the world, it would seem to some to make more sense to focus our culinary attentions on plants, because we would arguably get more energy per hectare for human consumption. Theoretically this should also mean fewer sentient animals would be killed to feed the ravenous appetites of ever more humans.

The Damage Done by Grain Production

But before scratching rangelands-produced red meat off the "good to eat" list for ethical or environmental reasons, let's test these presumptions.

Published figures suggest that, in Australia, producing wheat and other grains results in:

at least 25 times more sentient animals being killed per kilogram of useable protein,

more environmental damage, and

a great deal more animal cruelty than does farming red meat.

How is this possible?

Agriculture to produce wheat, rice and pulses requires clear-felling native vegetation. That act alone results in the deaths of thousands of Australian animals and plants per hectare. Since Europeans arrived on this continent we have lost more than half of Australia's unique native vegetation, mostly to increase production of monocultures of introduced species for human consumption.

Most of Australia's arable land is already in use. If more Australians want their nutritional needs to be met by plants, our arable land will need to be even more intensely farmed. This will require a net increase in the use of fertilisers, herbicides, pesticides and other threats to biodiversity and environmental health. Or, if existing laws are changed, more native vegetation could be cleared for agriculture (an area the size of Victoria plus Tasmania would be needed to produce the additional amount of plant-based food required).

Grazing can . . . cause significant damage such as soil loss and erosion. But it doesn't result in the native ecosystem "blitzkrieg" required to grow crops.

Most cattle slaughtered in Australia feed solely on pasture. This is usually rangelands, which constitute about 70% of the continent.

Grazing occurs on primarily native ecosystems. These have and maintain far higher levels of native biodiversity than croplands. The rangelands can't be used to produce crops, so production of meat here doesn't limit production of plant foods. Grazing is the only way humans can get substantial nutrients from 70% of the continent.

In some cases rangelands have been substantially altered to increase the percentage of stock-friendly plants. Grazing can also cause significant damage such as soil loss and erosion. But it doesn't result in the native ecosystem "blitzkrieg" required to grow crops.

This environmental damage is causing some well-known environmentalists to question their own preconceptions. British environmental advocate George Monbiot, for example, publically converted from vegan to omnivore after reading Simon Fairlie's expose about meat's sustainability. And environmental activist Lierre Keith documented the awesome damage to global environments involved in producing plant foods for human consumption.

In Australia we can also meet part of our protein needs using sustainably wild-harvested kangaroo meat. Unlike introduced meat animals, they don't damage native biodiversity. They are soft-footed, low methane-producing and have relatively low water requirements. They also produce an exceptionally healthy low-fat meat.

In Australia 70% of the beef produced for human consumption comes from animals raised on grazing lands with very little or no grain supplements. At any time, only 2% of Australia's national herd of cattle are eating grains in feed lots; the other 98% are raised on and feeding on grass. Two-thirds of cattle slaughtered in Australia feed solely on pasture.

To produce protein from grazing beef, cattle are killed. One death delivers (on average, across Australia's grazing lands) a carcass of about 288 kilograms. This is approximately 68% boneless meat which, at 23% protein equals 45kg of protein per animal killed. This means 2.2 animals killed for each 100kg of useable animal protein produced.

Producing protein from wheat means ploughing pasture land and planting it with seed. Anyone who has sat on a ploughing tractor knows the predatory birds that follow you all day are not there because they have nothing better to do. Ploughing and harvesting kill small mammals, snakes, lizards and other animals in vast numbers. In addition, millions of mice are poisoned in grain storage facilities every year.

Mice and Other Small Animals

However, the largest and best-researched loss of sentient life is the poisoning of mice during plagues.

Each area of grain production in Australia has a mouse plague on average every four years, with 500-1000 mice per hectare. Poisoning kills at least 80% of the mice.

You may dismiss snakes and lizards as cold-blooded creatures incapable of sentience, though they form pair bonds and care for their young. But what about mice?

At least 100 mice are killed per hectare per year (500/4 x 0.8) to grow grain. Average yields are about 1.4 tonnes of wheat/hectare; 13% of the wheat is useable protein. Therefore, at least 55 sentient animals die to produce 100kg of useable plant protein: 25 times more than for the same amount of rangelands beef.

Some of this grain is used to "finish" beef cattle in feed lots (some is food for dairy cattle, pigs and poultry), but it is still the case that many more sentient lives are sacrificed to produce useable protein from grains than from rangelands cattle.

There is a further issue to consider here: the question of sentience—the capacity to feel, perceive or be conscious.

You might not think the billions of insects and spiders killed by grain production are sentient, though they perceive and respond to the world around them. You may dismiss snakes and lizards as cold-blooded creatures incapable of sentience, though they form pair bonds and care for their young. But what about mice?

Mice are far more sentient than we thought. They sing complex, personalised love songs to each other that get more complex over time. Singing of any kind is a rare behaviour among mammals, previously known only to occur in whales, bats and humans.

Girl mice, like swooning human teenagers, try to get close to a skilled crooner. Now researchers are trying to determine whether song innovations are genetically programmed or whether mice learn to vary their songs as they mature.

Baby mice left in the nest sing to their mothers—a kind of crying song to call them back. For every female killed by the poisons we administer, on average five to six totally dependent baby mice will, despite singing their hearts out to call their mothers back home, inevitably die of starvation, dehydration or predation.

When cattle, kangaroos and other meat animals are harvested they are killed instantly. Mice die a slow and very painful death from poisons. From a welfare point of view, these methods are among the least acceptable modes of killing. Although joeys are sometimes killed or left to fend for themselves, only 30% of kangaroos shot are females, only some of which will have young (the industry's code of practice says shooters should avoid shooting females with dependent young). However, many times this number of dependent baby mice are left to die when we deliberately poison their mothers by the millions.

Replacing red meat with grain products leads to many more sentient animal deaths, far greater animal suffering and significantly more environmental degradation. Protein obtained from grazing livestock costs far fewer lives per kilogram: it is a more humane, ethical and environmentally-friendly dietary option.

The Ethical Diet

So, what does a hungry human do? Our teeth and digestive system are adapted for omnivory. But we are now challenged to think about philosophical issues. We worry about the ethics involved in killing grazing animals and wonder if there are other more humane ways of obtaining adequate nutrients.

Relying on grains and pulses brings destruction of native ecosystems, significant threats to native species and at least 25 times more deaths of sentient animals per kilogram of food. Most of these animals sing love songs to each other, until we inhumanely mass-slaughter them.

The challenge for the ethical eater is to choose the diet that causes the least deaths and environmental damage.

Former Justice of the High Court, the Hon. Michael Kirby, wrote that:

"In our shared sentience, human beings are intimately connected with other animals. Endowed with reason and speech, we are uniquely empowered to make ethical decisions and to unite for social change on behalf of others that have no voice. Exploited animals cannot protest about their treatment or demand a better life. They are entirely at our mercy. So every decision of animal welfare, whether in Parliament or the supermarket, presents us with a profound test of moral character".

We now know the mice have a voice, but we haven't been listening.

The challenge for the ethical eater is to choose the diet that causes the least deaths and environmental damage.

There would appear to be far more ethical support for an omnivorous diet that includes rangeland-grown red meat and even more support for one that includes sustainably wild-harvested kangaroo.

Even Small-Scale Vegetable Farming Requires Hunting Animals

Tovar Cerulli

Tovar Cerulli is a vegan-turned-hunter writer, speaker, and consultant.

> To live, we must daily break the body and shed the blood of Creation. When we do this knowingly, lovingly, skillfully, reverently, it is a sacrament. When we do it ignorantly, greedily, clumsily, destructively, it is a desecration.
>
> —*Wendell Berry,* The Gift of Good Land

The trouble started small: holes in the leaves of our squash seedlings.

Investigating, we discovered the little yellow-and-black-striped perpetrators. Cucumber beetles. Perhaps, compassionate vegans that we were, we would let them be. We could live with a few perforations, just as we had overlooked the woodchuck's depredations at Bird Cottage and the pinholes inflicted on our salad greens by flea beetles.

But soon the tiny squash plants—each with only a pair of tender, rounded leaves—were being stripped entirely.

So I started making forays before work each morning. That early, at fifty degrees, the beetles walked slowly and couldn't fly. I would find them, usually clinging to the undersides of the seedlings' leaves, pick them up between thumb and forefinger, and squish them one by one, their exoskeletons cracking, their innards staining my skin orange. Far better, I thought, to hunt them down like this than to spray those few plants with a toxic pesticide whose indiscriminate, invisible work would save me the gory morning task.

Cabbage moth larvae, though, were camouflaged. Their pale green caterpillar bodies blended into broccoli stalks almost perfectly and, once they got munching, they decimated the plants in a hurry. Researching our options, we decided on Bt (*Bacillus thuringiensis*), a bacterium used by organic farmers to target specific pests. When cabbage moth larvae ingest it, they die. We bought a little and sprayed it on the broccoli.

In 2000 the U.S. Fish and Wildlife Service estimated that 672 million birds are "directly exposed to pesticides" on American farmland each year.

Strict veganism prohibits eating honey, out of concern for bees. Beetle squishing and caterpillar poisoning were, I knew, beyond the pale. I was murdering insects.

Damage to the Land

More than a century ago, Howard Williams began his treatise on the history of vegetarianism by invoking the ancient Greek poet Hesiod, who valorized "the peaceful spirit of agriculture and mechanical industry" over "the spirit of war and fighting." But how peaceful is our tilling of the earth?

I knew enough about industrial food production to realize that it wasn't all endless acres of Edenic cultivation. Topsoil, for example, is being lost at an alarming rate. According to a 2006 study by Cornell University ecologist David Pimentel, erosion is stripping U.S. farmland of its dirt at ten times the rate of natural replenishment. And precious soil isn't all that gets washed downstream. Fertilizers also end up in our rivers, harming fish and other aquatic life. In high enough concentrations, nutrient-rich fertilizer runoff can maintain a cycle of phytoplankton blooms, depleting oxygen levels so severely that virtually nothing else can survive. Where the Mississippi dumps into the Gulf of Mexico, the seasonal dead zone had already grown to the size of New Jersey—even before the *Deepwater Horizon* oil spill of 2010 devastated the region.

And then there are pesticides. The recovery of the peregrine falcon notwithstanding, in 2000 the U.S. Fish and Wildlife Service estimated that 672 million birds are "directly exposed to pesticides" on American farmland each year. Some 67 million die immediately. Millions more die slowly. In Central and South America, where unregulated and highly toxic chemicals are sprayed and where many migratory birds go during North American winters, mortality rates are dramatically worse. Throughout the Americas alone, creatures smaller and less noticeable than birds are presumably killed by the uncounted billions.

Whatever we do to the planet, of course, we do to ourselves. As the earth loses topsoil, we're rapidly losing arable land. Windblown dust from eroding farmland pollutes the air we breathe and carries diseases like tuberculosis and anthrax. And it doesn't take an advanced degree in toxicology to figure out that pesticides don't do the human body any favors. Sixty-seven million birds make an awfully big pile of canaries in the proverbial coal mine.

Yet I knew, too, that agriculture didn't have to be so brutal. Soil erosion could be prevented by planting cover crops, such as rye or wheat. There were alternatives to chemical fertilizers and pesticides. Whenever possible, Cath and I opted for organic foods, minimizing our diet's chemical footprint. We ate close to home, buying food grown by small-scale, local farmers: no need to truck the produce cross-country, no gratuitous plastic packaging, and, thankfully, no massive combines mincing rabbits, rodents, birds, and birds' nests as they worked the fields each season. (Studies suggest that grain harvesters wipe out between 50 and 75 percent of populations in a long list of field-dwelling species.) Though much of our food still came from afar—greens and fruit in winter, tofu and other products year-round—"local" and "organic" were my watchwords. They signified harmlessness, shoring up my decade-long vegan diet, reassuring me that agriculture was, at its roots, a gentle blessing on the land: a backyard vegetable patch stretching out into those amber waves of grain.

Whenever any of us sit down for breakfast, lunch, dinner, or a snack, it's likely that deer were killed to protect some of the food we eat and the beverages we drink.

Deer

What got my attention was the deer. I was reading Richard Nelson's *Heart and Blood: Living with Deer in America.* Deer, I learned, eat just about everything farmers grow. They eat greens and pumpkins, corn and wheat, cranberries and carrots, avocadoes and wine grapes. They have a particular fondness for soybeans, used to make tofu, soy milk, and many other nonmeat, nondairy products sold in vegetarian-friendly stores around the country. They damage apple, plum, pear, cherry, and almond crops, often killing young trees. Individual farmers can sustain tens of thousands of dollars' worth of crop damage in a year; in many states, total annual losses run into the tens of millions.

In states where agriculture is a major sector of the economy, wildlife agencies have to keep the whitetail population down to a reasonable level. Often, that means encouraging hunters to shoot a lot of deer during hunting seasons. It also often means issuing special permits to farmers, allowing them to kill deer in other seasons, day or night. And farmers do kill them. By the thousands.

This isn't just out in the agricultural breadbasket of the American Midwest. Nelson interviewed an organic farmer in northern California who grew specialty greens for upscale restaurants and grocery stores in San Francisco. A few times a year, the farmer had to shoot a deer. Because he didn't like killing, sometimes he would cut the deer open and drag it around the perimeter of the field with a tractor, leaving plenty of blood to scare other deer away. Most years, he didn't have to kill more than five. In Westchester County [New York], just an hour north of Manhattan, another farmer gave Nelson a more startling figure: On his farm, they sometimes shoot ten in a single night. And still the crop damage continues. Nelson's summary of the situation brought me up short:

> Whenever any of us sit down for breakfast, lunch, dinner, or a snack, it's likely that deer were killed to protect some of the food we eat and the beverages we drink. . . . Everyone in modern North America who lives each day on agricultural foods belongs to an ecological network that necessarily involves deer hunting.

Deer are, he reports, "a fundamental part of our personal ecology. In this sense, the blood of deer runs through our veins as surely as we take bread and wine at our table."

I tried to keep that knowledge at bay. I told myself that those were bigger farms, far away, and that we weren't getting produce from those places. I was wrong.

In the end, I had to consider Joey, the kindly organic farmer whose veggies travel less than a mile to the produce display of the crunchy local food co-op—in whose fields Cath and I have often picked luscious strawberries. You'd be hard-pressed to find a gentler, more conscientious steward of the land. Ask him about deer, though, and he'll tell you: "I've got a few guys on call. When there's too much damage, they come and plug one and we share the venison." Or ask about wood-chucks: "I smoke-bomb their burrows constantly. Preemptively. A tunnel in a sandy bank right next to a kale field? Someone's going to move into that!"

Damn. I didn't want Bambi and Chuckie getting plugged and bombed as part of my "personal ecology."

Before long, though, I began to see that these deaths were among agriculture's lesser impacts, constituting only a fraction of the story. All it took was a few years working as a logger: work that grounded me in the local landscape and opened my eyes to its history. . . .

Regardless of whether the farming was done well or poorly, its initial establishment in all those places had required conquest, eviction of the creatures that lived there before, and conversion of the land to a new use.

After a day in the woods, a day of felling trees this way and that, leaving piles of hacked-off limbs everywhere I went, I would drive home past cornfields. I would return to the clearing where our house stands, to the placid scene of the flower and vegetable gardens Cath and I had built. And I would wonder: Is it neatness—the even regularity of raised beds and tilled rows, of summer corn and autumn stubble—that makes gardening and farming appear so much more benign than logging?

With a broader view of the landscape and our history here, I could look out across the Winooski and North Branch valleys and recognize the obvious. Every acre of agricultural land I had ever seen—every cow or sheep pasture, every wheat or soybean or vegetable field—was once forest, wetland, prairie: another kind of land. Regardless of whether the farming was done well or poorly, its initial establishment in all those places had required conquest, eviction of the creatures that lived there before, and conversion of the land to a new use. And maintaining it required constant defense against nature's efforts at reclamation.

That helped me understand something else I had seen as a boy. In the Vermont Historical Society museum, near the capitol in downtown Montpelier, is a big glass case. In the case stands a mountain lion. It is said to be the last cougar—or catamount, as we call them here—killed in Vermont, shot near the town of Barnard on Thanksgiving Day, 1881. As a boy, looking up at the big cat, I had grasped the immediate cause of its death: the man in the photograph, Alexander Crowell, sharp nosed and bearded, dressed in dark suit and hat, firearm cradled in the crook of his arm. And I had taken catamount hunting to be what extirpated the species from the state.

Loss of Habitat

In one sense, I had been right. Catamounts, like wolves, were indeed killed by men with guns, men who hated large predators for the danger they posed to livestock. Yet, despite the establishment of bounties in 1779 and the popularity of organized hunts, both species persisted in the state for decades.

What sounded the final death knell was loss of habitat. As expanses of forest were broken up, these predators' hunting territories shrank. Simultaneously, their primary food source—the white-tailed deer—was being driven to the brink of extinction by the same factors: overhunting and habitat loss. It is no coincidence that Vermont's remaining populations of wolves, catamounts, and deer all plunged precipitously in the first half of the nineteenth century when agricultural deforestation was at its peak. Only a few large predators survived the height of the merino's reign. And even those few were eventually hunted down, mainly for preying on the state's remaining sheep. There were, after all, virtually no deer left for wolf or catamount to eat. The "savage beast" shot by Crowell in 1881 had, according to a local newspaper report, "killed many sheep and lambs in different parts, and the people in this vicinity greatly rejoice at his death."

No doubt predators feasted on plenty of individual sheep. But the merino population as a whole was instrumental in wiping wolf and catamount off the landscape entirely.

Hiking in the woods late one summer, I turned off a hillside logging road toward a break in an old stone wall. Almost to that breach of tumbled stones, I glanced up for some reason. Four eyes locked with mine. Fifteen feet off the ground, two house-cat-sized felines clung to the bark of a nearby maple, one on each side of the trunk: kittens, all fuzzy from ruffed necks to stub tails.

Regardless of what I did, whether I liked it or not, I had an impact. No matter what I ate, habitat had already been sacrificed. No matter what I ate, animals would be killed.

They were bobcats, the catamount's much smaller cousin. They stared. I stared back. Though not rare in Vermont, bobcats are seldom seen in broad daylight, and such a close encounter with a pair of kittens was extraordinary. I gave myself an emphatic mental kick for not having a camera in my pocket.

When the spell broke, one kitten, then the other, leapt to the ground and vanished into cover. I caught a glimpse of one as it pranced from stone to stone along the top of the wall, then paused to look around, perhaps for its mother. She must have been close by.

Only later did I reflect on the spot. Though adaptable—and apparently tolerant of the occasional untidy passage of logging equipment through that timberland—bobcats prefer forest habitat. Neither they nor their main prey, snowshoe hares, thrive amidst intensive agriculture. The kittens would not have been there if that old stone fence still divided two pastures.

The mere fact of living, I had begun to realize, linked me to larger webs of life and death. Regardless of what I did, whether I liked it or not, I had an impact. No matter what I ate, habitat had already been sacrificed. No matter what I ate, animals would be killed.

Even while gardening within the confines of our deer- and woodchuck-proof fence, innocence was out of reach. The sandy soil, which I had ruthlessly stripped of grasses, wildflowers, and tree roots, needed all the organic matter it could get, so we imported compost by the truckload, compost made from the manure of chickens, horses, and cows. Now and then—shoveling the dark, rich stuff out of the back of my pickup—I would notice a knobby, light-colored chunk and pause to examine it. A fragment of bone. Perhaps the tip of a dairy cow's tibia.

We weren't eating animals, but our vegetables were.

CHAPTER 4

Is a Vegetarian Diet Beneficial for Health?

Vegan Diets Are Good
for Athletes

Scott Jurek

Scott Jurek is a vegan, ultramarathon runner, and author of Eat
and Run: My Unlikely Journey to Ultramarathon Greatness.

I run hundred-mile races. I eat only plants and vegetables.
Each of those sentences might shock some people. Read together, they might shock a whole lot of people.

What might shock them even more is to learn that I decided—with quite a few concerns—to change my diet just a
few months before the most important race of my life, at a
time when my workouts and recovery time were critical, in an
event that I knew might define my career.

An Unlikely Champion, an Unlikely Vegan

There is no more fabled trail footrace in North America than
The Western States 100 Mile Endurance Run. It attracts the
strongest trail runners in the country and offers some of the
most punishing terrain. Veterans puke and occasionally pass
out. More than a few are told to stop by doctors who wait at
medical check points on the course. Only one non-Californian
had ever won the men's division. The champion usually spent
a lot of time training in the mountains. The five years before I
entered, the champion lived in the mountains. His house was
next to the course. Though I wanted to be a great runner, and
though I knew I had to compete against the best in order to
test myself, the fact is, I had never won even a single 100 mile
race. And I grew up in Minnesota. The flatlands.

I was a total longshot, an unlikely champion.

I was an even more unlikely vegan.

When I was ten my dad had bought me a 22 caliber rifle with a polished walnut handle and a barrel made from burnished steel. His instructions were simple: If I wounded an animal, I killed it. If I killed it, I skinned it, gutted it, and ate it. We often had venison for dinner. By the time I was in sixth grade, I could yank a batch of Walleye from a lake after lunch, clean them, roll them in breadcrumbs, fry them in butter and devour them before sunset.

I loved roast pork, baked chicken and broiled steak. During high school I worked as a short order cook at a place called the Dry Dock Bar. My specialty was a kick ass Philadelphia Cheese Steak. In college, my roommate and I spent many a night on our back porch, feet on the banister, barbecued brats or burgers in our mitts, downing a tin of Planter Cheese Balls and a box of Malted Milk Balls in a single sitting. My nickname was the Grill Master.

It wasn't just meat. I loved fast food. I grew up in the country, and there were times when we had to shop with food stamps, and I ate government cheese. Restaurants were for birthdays. So being able to buy a burger—or chicken sandwich—whenever I wanted felt like freedom.

I was an athlete, and I was committed to protein, and what I thought was the fastest way to get it—through eating dead animals.

I started to cut down on meat and to ramp up on fruit and vegetables when I was in physical therapy school, influenced by my reading—especially Andrew Weil, MD, and Howard Lyman, my friends (a guy named Hippie Dan, aka The Unabaker, showed me the joys of wheatgrass and whole grain bread and talked a lot about solar energy and minimizing our carbon footprint) and the illness I saw every day in my work as a physical therapist. Along with the illness, I saw a lot of processed food and meat. I suspected there was a connection.

I learned that the three most common causes of death in our country—heart disease, cancer, and stroke—have all been linked to the standard Western diet, rich in animal products, refined carbohydrates, and processed food.

Even as I made the transition from Grill Master to vegetarian diet, I had reservations. One was money. For a backwoods boy from Minnesota, the idea of pricey groceries was anathema. When my girlfriend would show up with organic apples, or milk, and I would see the price tag, I went berserk. I'd yell, "You paid how much for that?! What's in it, gold dust?!"

Another concern was performance. I was an athlete, and I was committed to protein, and what I thought was the fastest way to get it—through eating dead animals.

My third worry was taste. Even after giving up meat, I was reluctant to let go of dairy. My sweet tooth was enormous. Cheese pizza never let me down.

So it turns out, an athlete, even one who trains up to eight hours a day, can do just fine with a plant-based diet.

Still, when I considered the increased stress to my kidneys, not to mention the chemicals and hormones injected into the country's food supply and the environmental degradation caused by cattle farms, the decision was easier. I even cut out fish when I realized that unless I caught it myself, in a body of water I knew was clean, I was likely going to be getting some hormones and other chemicals along with my salmon.

So that was it. No meat. No chicken. No fish. No dairy. No animal products of any kind. During my life, once I committed to something, I was all in. (That's a trait I share with many ultra-runners).

So even though I was about to compete in the toughest race of my life, even though I'd be running against men who trained year round in the mountains, and even though I didn't know whether the theoretical benefits of an animal-free diet would translate into a winning time, or if I would have to drop out from exhaustion, I went totally vegan.

The Payoff

Five months later, I shot off the starting line and into the lead. "He'll fade," I heard volunteers mutter at aid stations. "Wait until the champ catches him, then he's toast," I heard others whisper. "The tall guy went out too fast," specatators said. "Typical rookie mistake." For 90 miles, I heard people predict that "the flatlander" would soon collapse. But the last 10 miles there were only cheers. I led the entire race, from start to finish. I won that Western States, and the six after, setting a course record along the way. I won the 135-mile Badwater Ultramarathon, run in 125 degree heat through Death Valley, setting a record there, too. I even raced (and eventually defeated) the greatest member of the legendary Tarahumara Indians in Mexico's Copper Canyons. I won a lot of other races, too, including the 153-mile Spartathlon from Athens to Sparta and the Hardrock 100, the most difficult one hundred mile trail race in the world.

My performance wasn't the only thing that improved.

When I went vegan, my blood pressure and triglycerides levels dropped to all time lows, and my HDL, or "good" cholesterol shot up to an all-time high. I had virtually no joint inflammation, even after miles of pounding trails and roads, and on the rare occasions I sprained an ankle or fell and whacked my elbow or wrist, the soreness left faster than it ever had before.

So it turns out, an athlete, even one who trains up to eight hours a day, can do just fine with a plant-based diet. It also turns out that spending a little more time and money to eat healthy is incredibly cost effective; I think of a plant based diet as essentially the cheapest health insurance around. Being vegan wasn't a matter of subtraction, but addition. I discovered foods I had never known existed and experienced flavors and textures I had never imagined. Have you ever tasted a juicy lentil mushroom burger, or a savory bowl of veggie chili? If not, you should.

That's something to think about: A delicious, affordable diet that will make you healthier and support the most difficult physical challenges you could ever encounter. Now that's shocking.

A Plant-Based Diet Has Impressive Benefits

Sharon Palmer

Sharon Palmer is a registered dietitian, food and nutrition writer, and plant-based nutrition expert.

Recent findings indicate that instead of a meat-heavy diet, you're better off focusing on plants—whole grains, legumes, vegetables, fruits, nuts, seeds and soy.

People who eat a plant-based diet live longer, have less cancer and heart disease, weigh less, and have healthier diets. They even have a lower carbon footprint. These were the impressive findings from the landmark study Adventist Health Study-2 (first announced at the International Congress of Vegetarian Nutrition at Loma Linda University, Loma Linda, CA., February, 2013).

Adventist Health Study

What's so special about the Adventist Health Study? AHS-2 is the culmination of more than 50 years of research conducted at Loma Linda University on members of the Seventh-day Adventist religious denomination. The Adventists garnered interest among researchers due to their healthful lifestyle, which includes abstinence from cigarettes and alcohol, and high rates of vegetarianism—35 percent are vegetarian, compared to about four percent in the general population.

Within this group is a wide range of dietary patterns, from strict vegan to non-vegetarian, making this group a researcher's dream—scientists are able to study the effects of dietary patterns without the impact of other factors, such as smoking and alcohol.

The first Adventist Health Study (AHS-1, 1974–1988) examined risk of cancer and cardiovascular disease among 34,000 people. AHS-2, with 96,000 Adventist participants, was even more ambitious: Beginning in 2002, scientists at Loma Linda University compared the impact of various diet patterns within the same study population, making it one of the most comprehensive diet studies ever conducted. Data was gathered as subjects from all over the U.S. and Canada completed 50-page questionnaires about diet, lifestyle, and health.

The definition of a plant-based diet is not rigid; it simply means a diet that focuses on plants. Thus, someone who eats small amounts of animal foods can fit within this definition, as can someone who is a strict vegan and eats no animal foods. What makes AHS-2 unique is that scientists examined the effects of different plant-based diets within the study population. The five diet patterns in AHS-2 were broken down as follows:

1. Vegans who eat no animal products

2. Lacto-ovo vegetarians who eat no meat, but do eat eggs or dairy foods or both

3. Pesco-vegetarians who eat fish, but other meats one or fewer times per month

4. Semi-vegetarians who eat meats aside from fish occasionally, but less than weekly

5. Non-vegetarians who eat meats aside from fish at least one time per week

Plant-Based Eaters Eat Differently

Until this study, there was little knowledge about the daily intake of plant-based eaters. Gary Fraser, PhD, MPH, who led the AHS-2 research team at Loma Linda University, spoke about the study findings—both published and unpublished—at the Congress. He reported that for many years, researchers were convinced that various types of vegetarian diets were responsible for only moderate differences in health outcome, because there was inadequate research on plant-based diets.

For many health outcomes, a progressively beneficial relationship was observed between the dietary patterns, with vegan providing the best benefit compared with non-vegetarian.

But in AHS-2, "We saw huge differences in food intake among the different vegetarian dietary patterns," said Fraser. Fraser reported many interesting observations about various dietary patterns, including:

•Plant protein. Soy protein and plant protein intake is much greater in vegans than in non-vegetarians.

•Omega-3 fatty acids. While the omega-3 fatty acids EPA (eicosapentaenoic acid) and DHA (docosahexaenoic acid) intake is much lower among vegans and vegetarians, the plant omega-3 fatty acid ALA (alpha-linolenic acid) is higher in this group (about 2 grams per day), and higher levels of EPA and DHA are found in their body fat, suggesting high intake of plant omega-3s may result in higher levels in the body.

•Saturated fat. Intake is very low in vegans.

•Micronutrients. Beta-carotene and vitamin C intake is much higher in vegans. Vitamin B12 intake in vegans is low, but they often supplement this nutrient. Iron intake is good for vegans through the diet, as they don't typically supplement this nutrient.

•Calcium intake is very low in vegans, but not in lacto-ovo vegetarians.

Plant-Based Diets Offer Benefits

As the scientists began to compare the health outcomes of the various diet patterns in AHS-2, they saw something intriguing. For many health outcomes, a progressively beneficial relationship was observed between the dietary patterns, with vegan providing the best benefit compared with non-vegetarian, followed by lacto-ovo vegetarian, pesco-vegetarian, and semi-vegetarian.

In other words, the more plant-based the diet, the greater the benefit. Fraser presented the following findings:

1. Weight. A progressive weight increase was seen from a vegan diet toward a non-vegetarian diet. "The average body mass index (BMI) for vegans was 23.6, lacto-ovo vegetarians 25.7, pesco-vegetarians 26.3, semi-vegetarians 27.3, and non-vegetarians 28.8," said Fraser. BMI over 25 is overweight; over 30 is obese.

2. Cardiovascular disease. The same trend was observed for cardiovascular disease markers, such as levels of cholesterol, and incidence of high blood pressure and metabolic syndrome, with the vegan dietary pattern offering the lowest risk compared with non-vegetarian.

3. Type 2 Diabetes. Prevalence of type 2 diabetes among vegans (2.9 percent) and lacto-ovo vegetarians (3.2 percent) was half that of non-vegetarians (7.6 percent), reported Fraser, who also noted that the same trend prevailed in fasting blood glucose levels.

4. Inflammation. A similar trend, progressing from vegan to non-vegetarian, was observed for C-reactive protein, a measure of inflammation, which is considered a root of chronic disease.

5. Cancer. Fraser reported, "For overall cancer, all vegetarians (vegans plus lacto-ovo vegetarians) had an 8 percent reduction in risk, and vegans did best of all. For gastrointestinal cancers, vegetarians as a group had 24 percent reduction in risk, and in particular lacto-ovo vegetarians did the best. For

respiratory system cancers, the vegetarian group had a 23 percent reduction in risk. In female cancers, vegans did the best in reduced risk."

6. Longevity. "Death rates rise across the dietary groups, from vegans to non-vegetarians," said Fraser. There was a 12 percent reduction in risk of all-cause mortality in all vegetarians combined versus non-vegetarians, with a reduction in risk of 15 percent in vegans compared with non-vegetarians, nine percent in lacto-ovo vegetarians, 19 percent in pesco-vegetarians, and eight percent in semi-vegetarians.

7. Healthy behaviors. Compared to non-vegetarians, vegans and vegetarians watch less television, sleep more, and consume more fruits, vegetables, and low-glycemic foods and less saturated fat.

Carbon Footprint

Vegetarian diets are also more sustainable, according to Joan Sabate, MD, DrPh, Chair of Nutrition at Loma Linda University. According to a life cycle assessment applied to the AHS-2 data, Sabate reported that the greenhouse gas emissions for a vegan diet are 41.7 percent lower compared with non-vegetarians; lacto-ovo vegetarians are 27.8 percent lower, pescatarians are 23.8 percent lower, and semivegetarians are almost 20 percent lower.

Meat-Based Diets Improved Human Intelligence

Christopher Joyce

Christopher Joyce is a science correspondent for National Public Radio (NPR).

Our earliest ancestors ate their food raw—fruit, leaves, maybe some nuts. When they ventured down onto land, they added things like underground tubers, roots and berries.

It wasn't a very high-calorie diet, so to get the energy you needed, you had to eat a lot and have a big gut to digest it all. But having a big gut has its drawbacks.

"You can't have a large brain and big guts at the same time," explains Leslie Aiello, an anthropologist and director of the Wenner-Gren Foundation in New York City, which funds research on evolution. Digestion, she says, was the energy-hog of our primate ancestor's body. The brain was the poor step-sister who got the leftovers.

"What we think is that this dietary change around 2.3 million years ago was one of the major significant factors in the evolution of our own species," Aiello says.

That period is when cut marks on animal bones appeared—not a predator's tooth marks, but incisions that could have been made only by a sharp tool. That's one sign of our carnivorous conversion. But Aiello's favorite clue is somewhat ickier—it's a tapeworm. "The closest relative of human tapeworms are tapeworms that affect African hyenas and wild dogs," she says.

So sometime in our evolutionary history, she explains, "we actually shared saliva with wild dogs and hyenas." That would have happened if, say, we were scavenging on the same carcass that hyenas were.

But dining with dogs was worth it. Meat is packed with lots of calories and fat. Our brain—which uses about 20 times as much energy as the equivalent amount of muscle—piped up and said, "Please, sir, I want some more."

Carving Up the Diet

As we got more, our guts shrank because we didn't need a giant vegetable processor any more. Our bodies could spend more energy on other things like building a bigger brain. Sorry, vegetarians, but eating meat apparently made our ancestors smarter—smart enough to make better tools, which in turn led to other changes, says Aiello.

"If you look in your dog's mouth and cat's mouth, and open up your own mouth, our teeth are quite different," she says. "What allows us to do what a cat or dog can do are tools."

Tools meant we didn't need big sharp teeth like other predators. Tools even made vegetable matter easier to deal with. As anthropologist Shara Bailey at New York University says, they were like "external" teeth.

"Your teeth are really for processing food, of course, but if you do all the food processing out here," she says, gesturing with her hands, "if you are grinding things, then there is less pressure for your teeth to pick up the slack."

Our teeth, jaws and mouth changed as well as our gut.

A Tough Bite to Swallow

But adding raw meat to our diet doesn't tell the whole food story, according to anthropologist Richard Wrangham. Wrangham invited me to his apartment at Harvard University to explain what he believes is the real secret to being human. All I

had to do was bring the groceries, which meant a steak—
which I thought could fill in for wildebeest or antelope—and
a turnip, a mango, some peanuts and potatoes.

---

*It's not as if raw food isn't nutritious; it's just harder for
the body to get at the nutrition.*

As we slice up the turnip and put the potatoes in a pot,
Wrangham explains that even after we started eating meat,
raw food just didn't pack the energy to build the big-brained,
small-toothed modern human. He cites research that showed
that people on a raw food diet, including meat and oil, lost a
lot of weight. Many said they felt better, but also experienced
chronic energy deficiency. And half the women in the experi-
ment stopped menstruating.

It's not as if raw food isn't nutritious; it's just harder for
the body to get at the nutrition.

Wrangham urges me to try some raw turnip. Not too bad,
but hardly enough to get the juices flowing. "They've got a
tremendous amount of caloric energy in them," he says. "The
problem is that it's in the form of starch, which unless you
cook it, does not give you very much."

Then there's all the chewing that raw food requires.
Chimps, for example, sometimes chew for six hours a day.
That actually consumes a lot of energy.

"Plato said if we were regular animals, you know, we
wouldn't have time to write poetry," Wrangham jokes. "You
know, he was right."

One solution might have been to pound food, especially
meat—like the steak I brought. "If our ancestors had used
stones to mash the meat like this," Wrangham says as he dem-
onstrates with a wooden mallet, "then it would have reduced
the difficulty they would have had in digesting it."

But pounding isn't as good as cooking that steak, says
Wrangham. And cooking is what he thinks really changed our

modern body. Someone discovered fire—no one knows exactly when—and then someone got around to putting steak and veggies on the barbeque. And people said, "Hey, let's do that again."

Besides better taste, cooked food had other benefits—cooking killed some pathogens on food.

But cooking also altered the meat itself. It breaks up the long protein chains, and that makes them easier for stomach enzymes to digest. "The second thing is very clear," Wrangham adds, "and that is the muscle, which is made of protein, is wrapped up like a sausage in a skin, and the skin is collagen, connective tissue. And that collagen is very hard to digest. But if you heat it, it turns to jelly."

As for starchy foods like turnips, cooking gelatinizes the tough starch granules and makes them easier to digest too. Even just softening food—which cooking does—makes it more digestible. In the end, you get more energy out of the food.

Yes, cooking can damage some good things in raw food, like vitamins. But Wrangham argues that what's gained by cooking far outweighs the losses.

As I cut into my steak (Wrangham is a vegetarian; he settles for the mango and potatoes), Wrangham explains that cooking also led to some of the finer elements of human behavior: it encourages people to share labor; it brings families and communities together at the end of the day and encourages conversation and story-telling—all very human activities.

"Ultimately, of course, what makes us intellectually human is our brain," he says. "And I think that comes from having the highest quality of food in the animal kingdom, and that's because we cook."

So, as the Neanderthals liked to say around the campfire: *bon appetit.*

Not Everyone Benefits from a Vegetarian Diet

Sandro D'Amico

Sandro D'Amico is a physician at Four Rivers Naturopathic Clinic in Auburn, California.

So you want to eat healthy? No problem, just jump on the internet, check out a few health oriented diet websites and in no time you'll get all the information you need! Oh. . . . Uh . . . wait a minute, what's all that confusing, contradictory information . . . ?

If you haven't noticed, there's a battle for your allegiance going on right now all over the internet and on the shelves of bookstores everywhere. If you're not paying attention you may have missed it, but you're being exposed to it all the time. It's a battle about whether or not you should be eating meat.

Out of all the science and various good ideas about diet that have emerged in the last three decades, there are two camps who, at least for now, have become quite dominant in the national conversation about diet and health. Interestingly, at first glance, they appear to be almost diametrically opposed.

Vegan vs. Paleo

In one corner of the ring we have the "low carb" advocates, this would include followers of the Atkins diet, the South Beach diet, the Rosedale diet and the Paleo diet. In the other corner we have the vegans (i.e. no animal foods whatsoever). These would include followers of the ideas presented in the books "The China Study", "Diet for a New America" and the documentary film "Forks over Knives".

The Low carbers are well represented by the concept of the Paleo diet, whose essential argument is that we should be eating the way our cave person (please take note of my political correctness) ancestors ate. The word Paleo comes from the term paleolithic, which refers to pre-agriculture humans, i.e cave people. Proponents of the Paleo diet recommend eating plenty of meat, poultry, fish, eggs, fresh vegetables, fruits, nuts and seeds. What is notably missing here are grains, legumes and dairy products. Thankfully, the modern Paleo diet doesn't advocate eating grubs and insects, which I'm sure our hungry cave person ancestors ate when the circumstances dictated.

Vegans recommend eating a diet based entirely on plant foods: grains, legumes, vegetables, fruits, nuts, seeds and anything that is not part of, or does not come from an animal. What is missing here is meat, dairy and eggs.

The concept of veganism has been around for many years and was originally more associated with ethical and spiritual values, i.e. being kind to animals. In more recent years a strong stance has been taken amongst it's proponents that it is the healthiest diet for humans, and that eating meat is associated with all sorts of health problems. The promotion of this idea comes largely from a few authors, most notably John Robbins, author of "Diet for a New America" and more recently by T. Collin Campbell and Thomas Campbell who wrote the very popular book "The China Study".

Authors on both sides of this debate are starting from an emotional or philosophical viewpoint and then consciously or unconsciously finding evidence to support their position.

So, what's going on here? How can presumably intelligent and sincere health researchers come to such dramatically different conclusions? While I can't answer that question definitively, I can give an educated hunch: bias and selective reporting.

One of the greatest pitfalls in research is looking selectively at the evidence. If you are doing research on the health effects of ice cream, for instance, and you really love ice cream and don't want to stop eating it, you may find yourself searching out or giving more credence to evidence that makes positive assessments of ice cream (such as the study that suggests that regular ice cream consumption reduces osteoporosis in premenopausal women), and ignoring or giving less credence to evidence that ice cream isn't good for you (such as the fact that you get congested and lethargic every time you eat it). This is easy to do, consciously or unconsciously, and I have found myself doing it when researching various health topics that I had an emotional investment in.

My sense is that authors on both sides of this debate are starting from an emotional or philosophical viewpoint and then consciously or unconsciously finding evidence to support their position while ignoring or minimizing evidence that contradicts it.

Weighing In on the Paleo Diet

The argument that we should eat the same pre-agricultural foods that our ancestors ate for millennia makes a certain amount of sense. Our bodies evolved, in part, in response to the foods that were available during prehistoric times and so are arguably better adapted to them. Indeed, in evolutionary terms, there has simply not been enough time since the advent of agriculture about 12,000 years ago for any appreciable change to our digestive or metabolic processes. There has certainly not been enough time to adapt to the dramatic changes to our diet brought on by the onset of industrialization 200 years ago.

There is, however, some inconvenient evidence that contradicts the core Paleo assumption. There are a number of populations around the world currently and historically who have enjoyed excellent health, a lower incidence of chronic diseases, extremely low rates of obesity and in some cases, increased longevity who consume grains as a daily part of their diet. This would suggest that it is not grains in and of themselves that are harmful to human health, at least not for all people.

And, while certain health parameters such as energy, blood sugar and cholesterol levels do reliably improve when transitioning from a standard Western diet to a Paleo type diet (we see this regularly in our clinic), many broader health claims are made by proponents of the diet for which there is really no hard evidence, such as reduced risk of heart disease, cancer and increased longevity. (I'm not saying that the Paleo diet does not have these effects, just that we don't really know).

Weighing In on the Vegan Diet

Clearly there is something very appealing and noble about the idea of being able to sustain our health without causing suffering to other creatures. I can't, and wouldn't want to argue with that at all. The suggestion, however, that avoidance of all animal based foods is necessary, or even preferable to achieve optimal health is questionable, in my opinion.

Dr. Campbell's argument begins with mice. While his results are compelling, research has shown over and over again that mice are not human!

When the book "The China Study" came out several years ago, I read it and was initially very impressed and convinced by the author's essential arguments. T. Collin Campbell is a research scientist who did studies on mice given varying amounts of animal protein in their diets. He found that when mice ate more than 5% of their diet as animal protein (in the form of casein, an isolated protein from cow's milk) their incidence of cancer increased, furthermore, their rates of cancer increased in proportion to the amount of casein in their diet.

He was later involved in epidemiological research in China comparing a more traditional Chinese diet which contains high amounts of plant based foods and very small amounts of animal based foods with a more modern western diet. It was found that rates of cancer and certain other diseases were lower in people eating a traditional Chinese diet. Dr. Campbell's conclusion is that it is the percentage of animal based foods in the diet which are responsible for increased rates of cancer.

The more I thought about Dr. Campbell's conclusions, the more I was bothered. Dr. Campbell's argument begins with mice. While his results are compelling, research has shown over and over again that mice are not human! It is quite common, for instance, to see robust results in tests of therapeutic agents on mice or rats that do not later bear out in human studies. Furthermore, despite all the images we have seen in our lifetimes of mice eating cheese, casein is not the natural diet of mice! Mice in the wild primarily eat grains, seeds, berries and bugs.

Furthermore, people eating a traditional diet in China are more likely to be living in a rural environment and living a more traditional lifestyle overall. Individuals eating more meat and dairy products are likely to be urban dwellers. People in urban centers are often exposed to increased levels of stress, pollution, refined foods, loss of social support and disturbed sleep due to noise and light pollution. All of these may account for some of the differences in disease incidence that Dr. Campbell's team found.

In addition, it is well documented that Inuit people (historically called eskimos) living on their traditional diet, which consists almost entirely of animal products, such as fish, seal, whale meat and blubber, have extremely low rates of cancer, even in recent times. When they adopt more western diets, their cancer rates and other disease rates increase proportionately. In a similar vein, Weston Price, the famous dentist who travelled around the world studying groups of un-usually healthy people found that virtually all of them ate some meat, and some of them obtained a large percentage of their calories from dairy products.

What's Going on Here?

To begin with, proponents of both the Paleo diet and the ve-gan diet generally advocate eating whole, unprocessed foods. If one is eating a standard American diet, making that change alone will undoubtedly bring some health benefits, and for some people it will bring dramatic health benefits. What is true for all humans is that prior to about 200 years ago we were eating diets that consisted primarily of whole, unrefined foods. Diets of unprocessed, natural foods are nutrient dense, high in fiber, and very low in potentially toxic substances which can impair or derange metabolism.

Avoiding grains and carbohydrates does not, in and of it-self, make a diet healthy.

I do feel that both the vegan and Paleo camps are identify-ing real problems in our dietary landscape and offering some useful information. For me, the problem starts when a group of useful dietary principles are solidified into a block prescrip-tion for the entirety of humanity.

I have worked with a number of vegans (and vegetarians) who were sick specifically because their bodies could not maintain balance long term on a vegan or vegetarian diet. Vir-tually any naturopath can tell you stories about patients who's health improved dramatically when they started including some animal products, particularly meat, poultry and fish, into their diet. Having said that, there are some people who seem to do very well on a vegan or vegetarian diet.

I have also worked with people on a low carb diet who were living on pork chops, bacon and all sorts of low carb specialty foods and were quite unhealthy. Dr. Atkins, who started the low carb movement, had a heart attack later in life. Avoiding grains and carbohydrates does not, in and of itself, make a diet healthy.

The current vegan movement has made a number of important contributions. It has brought attention to ethical issues related to the treatment of animals. It has created a national conversation about the health implications of eating foods produced by modern farming methods.

Modern factory farms use massive feed lots where animals are fed a diet entirely unnatural to them (genetically modified corn) and kept in cramped quarters where they have to stand in their own manure and some of them are so sick that they can't even stand on their own feet. This is not only inhumane but factory farming produces meat, poultry and fish that comes from unhealthy animals and is high in inflammatory compounds that are associated with increased risk of heart disease and cancer. Beef, lamb and buffalo raised entirely on grass do not have these problems.

Advocates of the Paleo diet and other low carb diets have highlighted the connection between excessive consumption of refined carbohydrates and a variety of health conditions, including obesity, hypertension and diabetes. In addition, the Paleo diet in specific has promoted a diet based in whole, unprocessed foods, something the father of all low carb diets, the Atkins diet, lacked.

The Paleo and vegan diet movements have focused on what category of foods we should eat. The problem with that is that we are all individuals and have different needs from each other, and different needs at different times of our lives. Using our intelligence, being sensitive to the feedback our bodies give us and adjusting our habits accordingly can help us find a diet that will nourish and nurture us. This, of course, will provide an internal environment that is conducive to healing.

Vegetables Cause More Cases of Food Poisoning than Meat

NHS Choices

NHS Choices is the United Kingdom's leading health information service.

Can fruit and vegetables be dangerous? *The Mail Online* seems to think so. A story published on the website warns that: "Getting your five a day is responsible for half of all food poisoning cases."

The story comes from a decade-long US study of the sources of foodborne illnesses in the US. It estimates that nearly half of all foodborne illnesses were caused by fruit, nuts and vegetables, particularly green leafy vegetables. Meat and poultry accounted for around one in five cases.

The study highlights the important fact that any foodstuff, if it is improperly prepared or stored, can cause food poisoning.

The germs responsible for these illnesses attributed to leafy vegetables commonly include E. coli and the winter vomiting bug, norovirus. These highly contagious germs are often spread "hand-to-mouth" (usually through not washing hands properly after going to the toilet).

However, these results do not mean that fruit and vegetables are bad for you, only that it is crucial to have high standards of personal and food hygiene.

There are rules covering the hygiene requirements of environments and personnel involved in the preparation and handling of food in the UK [United Kingdom].

Meanwhile, in the home there are many ways you can help to stay safe, including washing your hands before handling

"Food Poisoning Warning Over Fruit and Veg," Behind the Headlines—Health News from NHS Choices, National Library of Medicine, www.ncbi.nlm.nih.gov.

and eating food, thoroughly washing raw fruit, vegetables and salads before eating, taking care over the storage of food and ensuring that meat for your weekend barbecue is thoroughly cooked.

The Research

The study was carried out by researchers from the US Centers for Disease Control and Prevention, which is funded by the US government. The study was published in the peer-reviewed open-access journal *Emerging Infectious Diseases*.

The Mail Online's headline appears to be confusing and perversely scaremongering, as it implies that eating five portions of fruit and vegetables increases your risk of food poisoning—a claim that is not supported by the study. A more useful headline would have explained the cause of the problem—poorly prepared, handled or stored fruit and vegetables can lead to food poisoning.

This frankly silly type of headline writing is a shame as the actual article is very well written and should be congratulated for highlighting the often ignored issue of "fruit and veg" associated food poisoning.

One challenge in preventing foodborne illness is to decide where to prioritise food safety efforts, when a number of different foods may be involved.

In this study, researchers aimed to calculate which specific foods and food groups were responsible for food poisoning outbreaks reported in the US between 1998 and 2008. They used this information to estimate the foods chiefly responsible for foodborne illness.

The authors point out that, despite advances in food safety, more than 9 million people suffer food poisoning in the US each year.

They say that one challenge in preventing foodborne illness is to decide where to prioritise food safety efforts, when a number of different foods may be involved (such as meat, fish or salad).

Attributing all illnesses to specific foods is challenging because most food pathogens are transmitted through a variety of foods and linking an illness to a particular food is rarely possible except during an outbreak.

Food poisoning can be caused by a range of different pathogens. These include bacteria (such as salmonella and E. coli), viruses (such as norovirus, known as the "winter vomiting" bug), chemicals, and parasites (such as cryptosporidium). In the UK, most cases of food poisoning are caused by bacteria or viruses.

Most cases of food poisoning are not serious, although they are usually unpleasant. Complications can occur in more vulnerable people, such as older people, and they may require admission to hospital, for example due to dehydration.

It is estimated that in the UK, food poisoning is to blame for 20,000 hospitalisations and 500 deaths every year.

For their study, the researchers used data on food poisoning outbreaks in the US reported to the US Centers for Disease Control and Prevention (CDC) from state and local health departments, through an established surveillance system.

These reports include the number of people taken ill, the suspected or confirmed cause of the outbreak (the pathogen or "bug"), the implicated food "vehicle" (the meal that caused the poisoning) and the identity of contaminated ingredients in that food.

They say that during 1998–2008, a total of 13,352 foodborne disease outbreaks, causing 271,974 illnesses, were reported in the US. Of these, they looked at 4,887 (37%) which were attributed to a particular food "vehicle" (source) and a single cause. They excluded 298 of these outbreaks because not enough information about the food "vehicle" was provided to categorise ingredients.

They obtained data on the estimated number of illnesses, hospitalisations and deaths for each outbreak.

The researchers then created 17 mutually exclusive food groups or "commodities":

- three for aquatic animals (fish, crustaceans and molluscs)

- six for land animals (dairy, eggs, beef, game, pork and poultry)

- eight for plants (grains and beans, oils and sugars, fruits and nuts, fungi, and leafy, root and vine-stalk vegetables)

[Researchers] found that norovirus ... caused the most outbreaks (1,419) and illnesses (41,257) in the US during the period analysed.

They also divided foods into those that were "simple" (containing ingredients from one group or commodity only (such as apple juice or fruit salad) and "complex" (containing ingredients from more than one commodity, such as apple pie (made from fruit, flour, sugar and dairy).

They then calculated the proportion of outbreak-associated illnesses transmitted by each food commodity, taking account of whether foods involved in the outbreaks were complex or simple. They then applied the percentages they derived from the data to the 9.6 million estimated annual illnesses in the US caused by food poisoning. They provided a range of estimates, using the most probable estimates in their results.

The Research Results

The researchers included 4,589 food poisoning outbreaks and 120,321 cases of food poisoning in their study. They found that norovirus (the most common cause of diarrhoea and vomiting in the UK and elsewhere) caused the most outbreaks (1,419) and illnesses (41,257) in the US during the period analysed.

Causes of foodborne illness

- plant commodities—fruits, nuts and vegetables—accounted for 46% of foodborne illnesses

- meat and poultry accounted for 22% of illnesses

- among all 17 commodities, more illnesses were attributable to leafy vegetables (2.2 million or 22%) than any other commodity

- after leafy vegetables, commodities linked to the most illnesses were dairy (1.3 million, 14%), fruits and nuts (1.1 million, 12%), and poultry (900,000, 10%)

Hospitalisations for food poisoning

- 46% (26,000) of annual hospitalisations were attributed to meat and dairy (land animals)

- 41% (24,000) were attributed to plant foods

- 6% (3,000) were attributed to fish and other seafood (aquatic animals)

- dairy foods accounted for the most hospitalisations, followed by leafy vegetables, poultry and vine stalk vegetables

Deaths from food poisoning

- an estimated 43% (629) deaths each year were attributed to meat (land animals), 363 (25%) to plant foods and 94 (6%) to fish and other seafood (aquatic animals)

- poultry accounted for the most deaths (19%) followed by dairy (10%), vine stalk vegetables (7%), fruit-nuts (6%) and leafy vegetables (6%)

They also say that plant foods accounted for 66% of viral illness, 32% of bacterial, 25% of chemical and 30% of parasitic illness.

The researchers point out that more illnesses were attributed to leafy vegetables (22%) than to any other commodity. In addition, illnesses associated with leafy vegetables were the second most frequent cause of hospitalisations (14%) and the fifth most frequent cause of death (6%). Efforts are particularly needed to prevent contamination of plant foods and poultry, they argue.

Reduce Your Risk

This large study of the possible sources of food poisoning in the US over a ten year period comes from a reputable source. However, as the authors point out, it can only give estimates as to the sources of food poisoning and it is also based on data before and up to 2008.

The findings of the study are of concern and a timely reminder of the crucial importance of food hygiene.

Since that time, patterns of food poisoning and the agents which cause it, may have changed. Also, its calculations are based on only a third of all food poisoning outbreaks in the US during the ten years covered.

It should also be noted that the findings may not apply to food poisoning trends in the UK.

Nevertheless, the findings of the study are of concern and a timely reminder of the crucial importance of food hygiene. The germs responsible for these illnesses attributed to leafy vegetables mostly include those highly contagious germs that are most often spread from the hand to the mouth, especially if you haven't washed your hands properly after going to the toilet.

While this study did not explore the causes of these outbreaks, the vegetables would have most likely been contaminated by the hands of people carrying these bacteria at any stage along the line of production, processing or preparation.

There are high standards covering the hygiene requirements of environments and personnel involved in the preparation and handling of food in the UK. And ensuring food is safe to eat is a legal responsibility of both those involved in food production and processing. However, you should be wary of being complacent about food hygiene.

You can reduce your risk by:

- always washing your hands before handling and eating food

- thoroughly washing raw fruit, vegetables and salads before eating

- ensuring produce such as fresh produce doesn't come into contact with raw meat

- ensuring that meat is thoroughly cooked

- when reheating items ensure that they are thoroughly heated through

- ensuring that meats, fish, dairy products and prepared meals are refrigerated, and not left standing in the room or outside (in hot temperatures, the time after which such food will become unsafe to eat will be less)

- observing use-by dates

Vegetarian Diets Are Not Healthy

Kris Gunnars

Kris Gunnars is a medical student, personal trainer, and blogger at AuthorityNutrition.com.

There is no one right way to eat for everyone.

We are all different and what works for one person may not work for the next.

I personally advocate consumption of *both* animals and plants and I think there is plenty of evidence that this is a reasonable way to eat.

However, I often get comments from vegans who think that people should eliminate *all* animal foods.

They frequently say that I'm giving out dangerous advice, that I must be corrupt and sponsored by the meat and dairy industry, or that I'm simply misinformed and need to read *The China Study*.

Really . . . I have *nothing* against vegans or vegetarians.

If you want to eat in this way for whatever reason and you are feeling good and improving your health, then great! Keep on doing what you're doing.

But I do have a *serious* problem when proponents of this diet are using lies and fear mongering to try and convince everyone else to eat in the same way.

I'm tired of having to constantly defend my position regarding animal foods, so I decided to summarize what I think are the key problems with vegan diets.

Here are 5 reasons why I think vegan (as in no animal foods *at all*) diets are a bad idea. . . .

1. Vegans Are Deficient in Many Important Nutrients

Humans are omnivores. We function best eating *both* animals and plants.

There are some nutrients that can only be gotten from plants (like Vitamin C) and others that can only be gotten from animals.

Vitamin B12 is a water soluble vitamin that is involved in the function of every cell in the body.

It is particularly important in the formation of blood and the function of the brain.

Because B12 is critical for life and isn't found in any amount in plants (except some types of algae), it is *by far* the most important nutrient that vegans must be concerned with.

In fact, B12 deficiency is very common in vegans, one study showing that a *whopping 92%* of vegans are deficient in this critical nutrient.

Two other nutrients that have been demonized by vegan proponents are saturated fat and cholesterol.

But B12 is just the tip of the iceberg . . . there are other lesser known nutrients that are only found in animal foods and are critical for optimal function of the body.

Here are a few examples:

Animal protein contains all the essential amino acids in the right ratios. It is important for muscle mass and bone health, to name a few. Vegans don't get any animal protein, which can have negative effects on body composition.

Creatine helps form an energy reservoir in cells. Studies show that vegetarians are deficient in creatine, which has harmful effects on muscle and brain function.

Carnosine is protective against various degenerative processes in the body and may protect against aging. It is found only in animal foods.

Docosahexaenoic Acid (DHA) is the most active form of Omega-3 fatty acids in the body and primarily found in animal foods. The plant form of Omega-3s, ALA, is inefficiently converted to DHA in the body.

Two other nutrients that have been demonized by vegan proponents are saturated fat and cholesterol.

Cholesterol is a crucial molecule in the body and is part of every cell membrane. It is also used to make steroid hormones like testosterone. Studies show that saturated fat intake correlates with increased testosterone levels.

Not surprisingly, vegans and vegetarians have much lower testosterone levels than meat eaters.

Bottom Line: Vegans are deficient in many important nutrients, including Vitamin B12 and Creatine. Studies show that vegans have much lower testosterone levels than their meat-eating counterparts.

Put simply, the Atkins diet had several important advantages while the Ornish diet performed poorly for all health markers measured.

---

2. There Are No Studies Showing That They're Better Than Other Diets

Despite what vegan proponents often claim, there are *no controlled trials* showing that these diets are any better than other diets.

They often claim that low-carb, high-fat diets (the opposite of vegan diets) are dangerous and that the evidence clearly shows vegan diets to be superior.

I disagree.

This has actually been studied in a high quality randomized controlled trial (the gold standard of science).

The A to Z study compared the Atkins (low-carb, high-fat) diet to the Ornish (low-fat, near-vegan) diet.

This study clearly shows that the Atkins diet causes greater improvements in pretty much *all* health markers, although not all of them were statistically significant:

The Atkins group lost more weight, 10.4 lbs, while the Ornish group lost only 5.6 lbs.

The Atkins group had greater decreases in blood pressure.

The Atkins group had greater increases in HDL (the "good") cholesterol.

The Atkins group had greater decreases in Triglycerides. They went down by 29.3 mg/dL on Atkins, only 14.9 mg/dL on Ornish.

Then the Atkins dieters were about *twice as likely* to make it to the end of the study, indicating that the Atkins diet was easier to follow.

Put simply, the Atkins diet had several important advantages while the Ornish diet performed poorly for all health markers measured.

Now, there are *some* studies showing health benefits and lower mortality in vegetarians and vegans, such as the Seventh-Day Adventist Studies.

The problem with these studies is that they are so-called observational studies. These types of studies can only demonstrate correlation, *not causation*.

The vegetarians are probably healthier because they are more health conscious overall, eat more vegetables, are less likely to smoke, more likely to exercise, etc. It has nothing to do with avoiding animal foods.

In another study of 10,000 individuals, where both the vegetarians and non-vegetarians were health conscious, there was *no difference* in mortality between groups.

One controlled trial showed that a vegan diet was more effective against diabetes than the official diet recommended by the American Diabetes Association.

However, a low-carb diet has also been studied for this purpose and led to much more powerful beneficial effects.

A vegan diet may be better than the typical low-fat diet recommended by the mainstream nutrition organizations, but pretty much *any diet* fits that description.

> *Bottom Line*: Despite all the propaganda, there isn't any evidence that vegan diets are any better than other diets. Most of the studies are observational in nature.

3. Proponents of Vegan Diets Use Lies and Fear Mongering to Promote Their Cause

Some vegan proponents aren't very honest when they try to convince others of the virtues of the vegan diet.

They actively use lies and fear mongering to scare people away from fat and animal foods.

Despite all the propaganda, there really isn't any evidence that meat, eggs, or animal-derived nutrients like saturated fat and cholesterol cause harm.

People who promote vegan diets should be more honest and not use scare tactics and lies to make people feel guilty about eating animal foods, which are perfectly healthy (if unprocessed and naturally fed).

I'd also like to briefly mention *The China Study* . . . which is the holy bible of veganism and apparently "proves" that vegan diets are the way to go.

This was an observational study performed by a scientist who was madly in love with his theories. He cherry picked the data from the study to support his conclusions and ignored the data that didn't fit.

The main findings of the China study have been *thoroughly debunked.*

I recommend you look at these two critiques:

Denise Minger: The China Study—Fact or Fallacy

Chris Masterjohn: What Dr. Campbell Won't Tell You About The China Study

---

Vegan proponents often use fear mongering and scare tactics in order to convince people not to eat animal foods.

Also . . . a new study from China came out very recently, directly contradicting the findings of the China study.

According to this study, men eating red meat had a lower risk of cardiovascular disease and women eating red meat had a lower risk of cancer.

> *Bottom Line*: Vegan proponents often use fear mongering and scare tactics in order to convince people not to eat animal foods. They frequently cite *The China Study* as evidence, which has been thoroughly debunked.

4. Vegan Diets May Work in the Short Term, for Other Reasons

If you look at vegan message boards, you will quickly find stories of people who have seen *amazing* health benefits on a vegan diet.

I've got no reason to believe that these people are lying.

But it's important to keep in mind that this is anecdotal evidence, which isn't science.

You will find the same kinds of success stories for pretty much any diet.

Then you'll also find tons of people saying they got *terrible results* on a vegan diet.

Personally, I think that vegan diets *can* have health benefits for a lot of people . . . at least in the short term, before the nutrient deficiencies kick in (which can be partly circumvented by supplementation).

However, I don't think this has *anything* to do with avoiding animal foods!

Vegan diets don't just recommend that people avoid animal foods. They also recommend that people avoid added sugars, refined carbohydrates, processed vegetable oils and trans fats.

Then they suggest that people stop smoking and start exercising. There are so many confounders here that can easily explain all the beneficial effects.

These are extremely unhealthy foods, that's something the vegans and I agree on. I personally think that avoiding *these foods* is what is causing the apparent benefits.

Our bodies are perfectly capable of digesting, absorbing and making full use of the many beneficial nutrients found in animal foods.

I am 100% certain that a plant-based diet that includes at least a little bit of animals (the occasional whole egg or fatty fish, for example) will be *much healthier* in the long-term than a diet that eliminates animal foods completely.

Bottom Line: Vegan diets also recommend that people shun added sugar, refined carbohydrates, vegetable oils and trans fats. This is probably the reason for any health benefits, not the removal of unprocessed animal foods.

5. There Is NO Health Reason to Completely Avoid Animal Foods

Humans have been eating meat for hundreds of thousands (or millions) of years.

We evolved this way.

Our bodies are perfectly capable of digesting, absorbing and making full use of the many beneficial nutrients found in animal foods.

It is true that *processed* meat causes harm and that it's disgusting the way "conventionally raised" animals are treated these days.

However, animals that are fed natural diets (like grass-fed cows) and given access to the outdoors are completely different.

Even though processed meat causes harm, which is supported by many studies, the same does NOT apply to natural, unprocessed meat.

Unprocessed red meat, which has been demonized in the past, really doesn't have any association with cardiovascular disease, diabetes or the risk of death.

It has only a very weak link with an increased risk of cancer and this is probably caused by excessive cooking, not the meat itself.

Saturated fat has also never been proven to lead to heart disease. A study of almost 350 thousand individuals found literally *no association* between saturated fat consumption and cardiovascular disease.

Studies on eggs show no effect either. Multiple long-term studies have been conducted on egg consumption, which are very rich in cholesterol, and found no negative effects.

The thing is that animal foods . . . meat, fish, eggs and dairy products for those who can tolerate them, are *extremely nutritious*.

They are loaded with high quality protein, healthy fats, vitamins, minerals and various lesser known nutrients that have important effects on health.

There may be ethical or religious reasons not to eat animals. . . . I get it. But there is *no scientifically valid health reason* to completely eliminate animal foods.

Take Home Message

At the end of the day, the optimal diet for any one person depends on a lot of things.

This includes age, gender, activity levels, current metabolic health, food culture and personal preference.

Vegan diets may be appropriate for some people, *not others*. Different strokes for different folks.

If you want to eat a vegan diet, then make sure to be prudent about your diet. Take the necessary supplements and read some of the books by the vegan docs, I'm sure they at least know how to safely apply a vegan diet.

If you're getting results, feeling good and are managing to stick to your healthy lifestyle, then that's great. If it ain't broken, don't fix it.

But don't use fear mongering and scare tactics to persuade people to join your cause and scare them away from perfectly healthy animal foods. That ain't cool.

Organizations to Contact

The editors have compiled the following list of organizations concerned with the issues debated in this book. The descriptions are derived from materials provided by the organizations. All have publications or information available for interested readers. The list was compiled on the date of publication of the present volume; names, addresses, phone and fax numbers, and e-mail and Internet addresses may change. Be aware that many organizations take several weeks or longer to respond to inquiries, so allow as much time as possible.

Academy of Nutrition and Dietetics
120 S Riverside Plaza, Suite 2000, Chicago, IL   60606
(800) 877-1600
website: www.eatright.org

The Academy of Nutrition and Dietetics is the world's largest organization of food and nutrition professionals. The group strives to improve the nation's health and advance the profession of dietetics through research, education, and advocacy. The organization focuses on food and nutrition research and offers scholarships and awards. Its website, EatRight.org, contains numerous papers on managing a healthy, nutritionally sound, vegetarian diet.

American Meat Institute (AMI)
1150 Connecticut Ave. NW, 12th Floor
Washington, DC   20036
(202) 587-4200 • fax: (202) 587-4300
website: www.meatami.com/

The American Meat Institute is a national trade association that represents companies that process 95 percent of red meat and 70 percent of turkey in the United States. AMI tracks and informs legislation, regulation, and media activity that impacts the meat and poultry industry and provides updates and analyses to its members to help them stay informed. In addition, AMI conducts scientific research through its foundation designed to help meat and poultry companies improve their plants and their products. The AMI website includes numerous publications, reports, videos, and other resources addressing such topics as the environment, animal health and welfare, and diet and health.

Animals and Society Institute (ASI)
2512 Carpenter Rd., Suite 202-A, Ann Arbor, MI   48108-1188
(734) 677-9240 • fax: (734) 677-9242
e-mail: info@animalsandsociety.org
website: www.animalsandsociety.org

The Animals and Society Institute is a nonprofit, independent research and educational organization working to advance the status of animals in public policy and promote the study of human-animal relationships. The group's objectives are to stop the cycle of violence between animal cruelty and human abuse, learn more about our complex relationship with animals, and promote new and stricter animal protection laws. The ASI website contains information about their events and links to educational resources and publications.

Compassionate Farming Education Initiative (CFEI)
PO Box 740911, Boynton Beach, FL   33474
(718) 607-0288
e-mail: kellisritter@compassionatefarming.org
website: www.compassionatefarming.org

The Compassionate Farming Education Initiative is a nonprofit organization based out of southeastern Florida. The goal of CFEI is to empower individuals to make educated decisions regarding the foods they consume, while recognizing their own global impact. CFEI is also working toward developing an online curriculum to educate the public about current factory farming practices, explain the health and environmental risks and traumas associated with these foods, and offer healthy plant-based alternatives that are flexible, affordable, and sustainable. Educational resources currently available on the CFEI website include online educational materials, pamphlets, and video resources.

Humane Farm Animal Care (HFAC)
PO Box 727, Herndon, VA   20172
(703) 435-3883
e-mail: info@certifiedhumane.org
website: http://certifiedhumane.org

Humane Farm Animal Care is an international nonprofit certification organization dedicated to improving the lives of farm animals in food production from birth through slaughter. Their goal is to improve the lives of farm animals by driving consumer demand for kinder and more responsible farm animal practices. The organization ensures certified producers comply with food safety and environmental regulations and processors comply with the American Meat Institute Standards, a standard written by Temple Grandin, a doctor and member of the HFAC Scientific Committee. HFAC's website contains information on the certification process, as well as a blog and news center.

People for the Ethical Treatment of Animals (PETA)
501 Front St., Norfolk, VA   23510
(757) 622-7382 • fax: (757) 622-0457
website: www.peta.org

People for the Ethical Treatment of Animals (PETA) is the largest animal rights organization in the world. PETA focuses its attention on factory farms, the clothing trade, laboratories, and the entertainment industry. It also works on issues related to cruelty to wildlife and domesticated animals. PETA seeks to achieve its goals through public education, cruelty investigations, research, animals rescue, legislation, special events, celebrity involvement, and protest campaigns. The group's website contains information on all its projects as well as substantial information on livestock farming and vegan diets.

US Department of Agriculture (USDA)

1400 Independence Ave. SW, Washington, DC   20250
(202) 720-2791
website: www.usda.gov/wps/portal/usda/usdahome

The US Department of Agriculture exists to provide leadership on food, agriculture, natural resources, rural development, nutrition, and related issues based on sound public policy, the best available science, and efficient management. The department's activities include expanding markets for agricultural products, enhancing food safety by taking steps to reduce the prevalence of foodborne hazards from farm to table, improving nutrition and health by providing food assistance and nutrition education, and managing and protecting public and private lands. The USDA website includes a blog, press releases, and other publications, as well as information on all its programs and services.

US Food and Drug Administration (FDA)

5100 Paint Branch Pkwy., College Park, MD   20740
(888) 463-6332
website: www.fda.gov

The US Food and Drug Administration is the government agency responsible for ensuring the quality and safety of all food and drug products sold in the United States. As such, the FDA regulates safety and truthful labeling of all food products, including dietary supplements (except for livestock and poultry, which are regulated by the US Department of Agriculture), venison and other game meat, bottled water, food additives, and infant formulas. FDA reports, as well as current information on food quality issues, are available on its website.

Vegan Action/Vegan Awareness Foundation

PO Box 7313, Richmond, VA   23221
(804) 577-8341 • fax: (804) 254-8346
e-mail: info@vegan.org
website: www.vegan.org

The Vegan Action/Vegan Awareness Foundation works to reduce animal suffering, minimize environmental impact, and improve human health by educating the public about the benefits of a vegan diet. The group also acts as the certifying organization behind the "Certified Vegan" logo. Vegan Action's website contains information on animal health, vegan diets, and other topics related to the vegan lifestyle.

Vegan Outreach

PO Box 1916, David, CA   95617-1916
website: www.veganoutreach.org

Vegan Outreach is a nonprofit organization working to expose and end cruelty to animals through the widespread distribution of informational booklets. The titles, available on its website, include *Why Vegan? Even if You Like Meat, Compassionate Choices*, and *Guide to Cruelty-Free Eating*. The organization's website also has practical information on vegan diets, such as information on meat, egg and dairy substitutes and recipes, and an e-mail newsletter and blog.

Vegan Resource Group (VRG)

PO Box 1463, Baltimore, MD   21203
(410) 366-8343
e-mail: vrg@vrg.org
website: www.vrg.org

The Vegan Resource Group is a nonprofit organization dedicated to educating the public on vegetarianism and the interrelated issues of health, nutrition, ecology, ethics, and world hunger. The group, which is made up of health professionals, activists, and educators, works with businesses and individuals to bring about healthy changes in schools, workplaces, and communities. Registered dietitians and physicians aid in the development of nutrition related publications and answer member and media questions about the vegetarian and vegan diet. In addition to publishing the *Vegetarian Journal*, VRG produces and sells cookbooks, pamphlets, and other publications through its website.

Vegetarian Society of the United Kingdom

Parkdale, Dunham Rd., Altrincham   14 4QG
  United Kingdom
0 (161) 925-2000 • fax: 0 (161) 929-9182
e-mail: info@vegsoc.org
website: www.vegsoc.org

The Vegetarian Society of the United Kingdom is an educational charity working to support, represent, and increase the number of vegetarians in the country. The group works with businesses, government agencies, policymakers, and professionals. It offers free advice and information for families, individuals, health professionals, and others, and it provides education to youth in the classroom and vegetarian cooking lessons though their Cordon Vert school. The society also runs National Vegetarian Week. The organization's website contains information on all of its projects as well as recent news and press releases.

Bibliography

Books

Charlotte
Biltekoff

Eating Right in America: The Cultural Politics of Food & Health. Durham, NC: Duke University Press, 2013

T. Colin
Campbell

Whole: Rethinking the Science of Nutrition. Dallas, TX: BenBella Books, 2013.

T. Colin
Campbell

The Low-Carb Fraud. Dallas, TX: BenBella Books, 2014.

Sherry F. Colb

Mind if I Order the Cheeseburger? And Other Questions People Ask Vegans. Herndon, VA: Lantern Books, 2013.

Nick Cooney

Veganomics: The Surprising Science on What Motivates Vegetarians, from the Breakfast Table to the Bedroom. Herndon, VA: Lantern Books, 2013.

Rip Esselstyn

My Beef with Meat: The Healthiest Argument for Eating a Plant-Strong Diet. New York: Grand Central Life & Style, 2013.

Safran Foer

Eating Animals. New York: Back Bay Books, 2011.

Gary L. Francione
and Anna
Charlton

Eat Like You Care: An Examination of the Morality of Eating Animals. Seattle, WA: CreateSpace Independent Publishing, 2013.

Melanie Joy — *Why We Love Dogs, Eat Pigs, and Wear Cows: An Introduction to Carnism.* San Francisco: Conari Press, 2011.

Yuson Jung, Jakob A. Klein, and Melissa L. Cadwell, eds. — *Ethical Eating in the Postsocialist and Socialist World.* Oakland, CA: University of California Press, 2014.

Lierre Keith — *The Vegetarian Myth: Food, Justice and Sustainability.* Oakland, CA: PM Press, 2009.

Victoria Moran — *Main Street Vegan: Everything You Need to Know to Eat Healthfully and Live Compassionately in the Real World.* New York: Tarcher, 2012.

Maureen Ogle — *In Meat We Trust: An Unexpected History of Carnivore America.* Boston: Houghton Mifflin Harcourt, 2013.

Kristin Ohlson — *The Soil Will Save Us: How Scientists, Farmers, and Foodies Are Healing the Soil to Save the Planet.* Emmaus, PA: Rodale Books, 2014.

John Robbins — *The Food Revolution: How Your Diet Can Help Save Your Life and Our World.* San Francisco: Conari Press, 2010.

Judith D. Schwartz — *Cows Save the Planet: And Other Improbable Ways of Restoring Soil to Heal the Earth.* White River, VT: Chelsea Green Publishing, 2013.

David Robinson Simon — *Meatonomics: How the Rigged Economics of Meat and Dairy Make You Consume Too Much—and How to Eat Better, Live Longer, and Spend Smarter*. San Francisco: Conari Press, 2013.

Arran Stephens — *The Compassionate Diet: How What You Eat Can Change Your Life and Save the Planet*. Emmaus, PA: Rodale Books, 2011.

Periodicals and Internet Sources

Dave Asprey — "Athletic Anti-Nutrition: What a Vegan Diet Really Did for Carl Lewis," *The Bulletproof Executive*, March 2012. www.bulletproofexec.com.

Amber Averitt — "Can Meatless Meals Be Healthier?," SurfKY.com, December 30, 2014. http://surfky.com/index.php/communities.

Vanessa Barford — "The Rise of Part-Time Vegans," *BBC News Magazine*, February 17, 2014. www.bbc.com/news.

Mark Bittman — "Rethinking the Meat-Guzzler," *New York Times*, January 27, 2008.

Daniel Brook — "The Planet-Saving Mitzvah: Why Jews Should Consider Vegetarianism," *Tikkun Magazine*, July/August 2009. www.tikkun.org.

Kiera Butler — "Steak or Veggie Burger: Which Is Greener?," *Mother Jones*, July/August 2010.

Marcel Dicke and Arnold Van Huis — "The Six-Legged Meat of the Future," *Wall Street Journal*, February 19, 2011.

Rob Dunn — "Human Ancestors Were Nearly All Vegetarians," *Scientific American*, July 23, 2012.

Jonathan A. Foley — "Can We Feed the World and Sustain the Planet?," *Scientific American*, November 2011.

Jonathan A. Foley et al. — "Solutions for a Cultivated Planet," *Nature*, October 20, 2011.

Jane Fynes-Clinton — "Fleshing Out a Distaste for Meat over World Vegetarian Day," *The Courier-Mail*, September 27, 2012.

Jane Fynes-Clinton — "Vegetarianism Debate Should Give Us All Food for Thought," *The Courier-Mail*, January 9, 2014.

James Hamblin — "Vegetarians and Their Superior Blood," *The Atlantic*, February 24, 2014.

Angela Haupt — "Me, Give Up Meat? Vegan Diets Surging in Popularity," *U.S. News & World Report*, July 24, 2012.

Laura June — "Your Meat Addiction Is Destroying the Planet (But We Can Fix It)," *The Verge*, August 13, 2013. www.theverge.com.

Nicolette Hahn Niman	"Eating Animals," *The Atlantic*, December 20, 2011.
Wesley J. Smith	"Vegetarians Less Healthy," *National Review*, April 2, 2014.
Paul Solotaroff	"In the Belly of the Beast," *Rolling Stone*, December 10, 2013.
Stephanie Strom	"Fake Meats, Finally, Taste Like Chicken," *New York Times*, April 2, 2014.
A.G. Sulzberger	"Meatless in the Midwest: A Tale of Survival," *New York Times*, January 10, 2012.
John Vidal	"10 Ways Vegetarianism Can Help Save the Planet," *The Observer*, July 17, 2010.
John Vidal	"Global Meat Production and Consumption Continue to Rise," Worldwatch Institute, October 11, 2011. www.worldwatch.org.

Index